Charpentiers et charpenterie

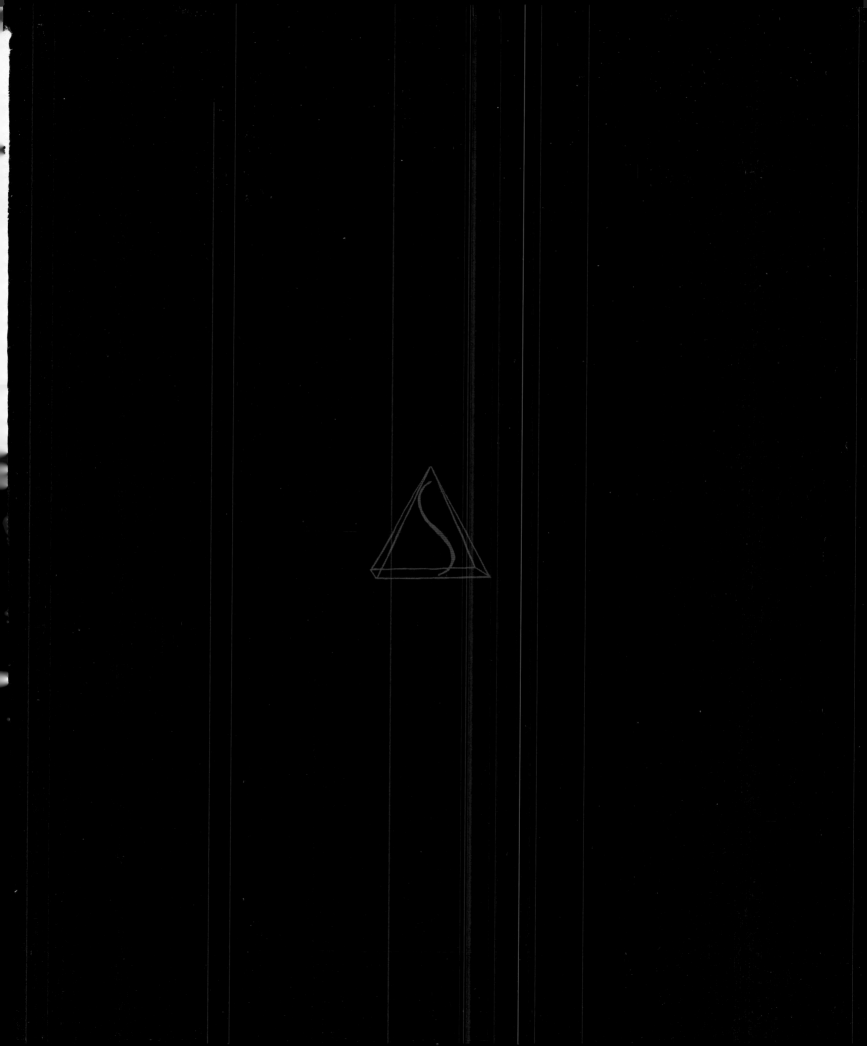

ANOTHER WORK IS POSSIBLE

Joshua A. Klein with *Charpentiers Sans Frontières*

Mortise & Tenon Inc.

—

SEDGWICK

AUTHOR
Joshua A. Klein

EDITOR
Michael Updegraff

ASSISTANT EDITOR
Jim McConnell

COPY EDITOR
Nancy Hiller

DESIGN DIRECTION
Frank Design Co.

DESIGNERS
Joshua A. Klein and Frank Design Co.

INDEXER
Michael Updegraff

PUBLISHER
Mortise & Tenon

ISBN: 978-0-9983667-7-7

Mortise & Tenon Inc.
14 Porcupine Ln
Sedgwick, ME
04676

Printed and bound in the United States of America
Signature Book Printing, www.sbpbooks.com

www.mortiseandtenonmag.com

Table of Contents

Dedicated to the late

William Coperthwaite (1930-2013),

who was the first to show me

that another way of life is possible.

PREFACE
A Celebration of Axe, Wood, Soil, and Sweat

"The human body, an organism that cannot see, hear, run, climb or swim very well, is the body of a generalist, for it can do all of these things to some extent. Now [in the factory system] it was forced into the role of a specialist… [and] personal expression has become the property of the artist, the hobbyist, the collector. The generalist in a simple society finds his satisfaction in his work; no other expression is necessary."

Christopher Williams — *Craftsmen of Necessity*

This book was written in the autumn of 2019 after the dust settled from the biggest project of my life – the hand-tool construction of a timber-framed blacksmith shop on my property in Maine. The pages that follow are intended as both an account of the event itself and a reflection on the lessons that this project symbolized for me. I am only one man, and therefore cannot pretend to speak for any other. I've discovered over the years that there are a myriad of valuable reasons people feel the inclination to pick up tools. And because of the diversity on the jobsite, it would be far-fetched to imagine that we all have the same reasons for working the way we do. So the takeaways in this book are my own. All that said, several of the carpenters sent me their own post-event reflections or the poetry selections they shared at our morning meetings as contributions to this book (many of which will be found as sidebars), and when I read them I realized that we all seem to be singing the same song – this timber frame embodies the joy of shared manual labor, a celebration of hand skills, and the beauty of meaningful and sensitive work. The thoughts written in these pages consciously echo the spirit of the conversations we shared during this week-and-a-half-long project. This book is a celebration of axe, wood, soil, and sweat as much as it is of reverence, compassion, and camaraderie.

It was Bill Coperthwaite's *A Handmade Life* that initially showed me how one might connect craftsmanship with life values. The first time I read this book, it sparked in me a passion to build a holistic life for my family – one in which craft, food, faith, love, work, and beauty are inextricably intermingled. What might patience have to do with the food on my family's dinner table? Why should passion fuel my daily work? How does the pursuit of humility affect my approach to my craft? These are the kinds of questions I have been pondering deeply since I read his book nearly 15 years ago.

Charpentiers Sans Frontières (CSF), "Carpenters Without Borders," is a France-based timber-framing team that my colleague, Michael Updegraff, and I were introduced to through our friend, Will Lisak, when he traveled to Romania with them in 2017 to work on a project. CSF travels the world to restore medieval masterpieces such as Château d'Harcourt, Château de Gaillon, and a 1491 barn in Aclou. This group, founded and led by ethnologist in the Ministry of Culture in Normandy, François Calame,

gathers carpenters from all over the world, most of whom have extensive experience in timber framing and historic carpentry.

The thing that impressed us so much about this group was that their work is done entirely by hand. Although Mike and I take a hand-tool-only approach to our furniture making, it was hard to envision constructing entire frames without the aid of sawmills, circular saws, or chain mortisers. Of course, we all know it was done that way for ages, but who in the 21st century would choose to do so? We were sure this must be an interesting group of people.

Through a series of events, two years after first hearing about them, *Charpentiers Sans Frontières* spent 11 days at our place in Maine in August 2019, and I got a firsthand view of the beauty of their work which is grounded in something more purposeful than economic expediency. I saw joyful, sweaty, skilled camaraderie that forged new relationships not only with people from many countries, but also with nature. This event so vividly brought together the most basic and human elements of life (food, work, song, community) that should never have been separated in the first place. I saw people working across borders as a model of a constructive alternative to the division, rivalry, and greed that pulls societies apart. CSF modeled for me the idea that if we're ever going to see change around us, it won't be by complaining – we need to show the world that another way is *actually possible.*

My life will never be the same after this event, and if I had only one goal for this book, it would be to share with you the beauty of the engaged and passionate life that these carpenters exemplified – one in which the work of the heart is just as important as the work of the hands.

– Joshua A. Klein, *Sedgwick, Maine*
DECEMBER 3RD, 2019

6

On the Origins of *Charpentiers Sans Frontières*

BY FRANÇOIS CALAME

"Over the years we've been doing this CSF work, we've sometimes witnessed the sudden extinction of authentic ancestral know-how, even while there has been a growing aspiration within our modern society towards the revival of manual trades."

François Calame

Detail of a craftsman mortising in the carpenter's yard. From Denis Diderot *Encyclopédie, ou Dictionnaire Raisonné des Sciences, des Arts et des Métiers*, Carpentry Plate 1.

OPPOSITE: France, Hez Forest, Oise. Croatian lumberjack Ivan Urbiha using his broadaxe with a crooked handle, the *stranak*.

PREVIOUS PAGE: Urbiha showing the use of his personal broadaxe, the *bradvil*.

Photos: François Calame.

In 1978 I became a rabbit. That is, I became a carpenter's apprentice, known facetiously as a "rabbit" among the *Compagnon* [1] carpenters in France. At that period in the French construction industry, we practiced what we called "traditional carpentry." Professional carpentry companies, whether *Compagnon*-run or not, were typically building robust frames using lapped-and-bolted members – an industrial technique called *moise* developed during the mechanization of the mid-19th century. [2] Categorically, our framing lumber came from industrial sawmills. The spirit of those times was a concern for rationalization of work, not with its poetics or romanticism. At that time, the term "traditional carpentry" simply meant that the work didn't make use of glue-lam framing, which was a new specialty.

The most "traditional" that this traditional carpentry got, as I saw in the workshop of the *Compagnon* René Turron (the Key of Hearts from Agen [3]) in Marseille, was creating simple lapped-and-bolted "latin trusses" (king post trusses) using salvaged timbers. [4] These were carefully dressed with an adze to give an impression of being hand-hewn, though the rippled surfaces looked more like that of a chocolate cream pie than a truly axe-hewn surface. My boss, an experienced and respected carpenter, had never tried hewing with an axe, nor seen it done. He was part of the post-war generation that fully embraced mechanization. Adze-dressing timbers was part of a neo-rustic fashion in the final third of the 20th century. We spent considerable time pulling nails from the salvaged beams – pity on him whose adze struck a nail buried in a misleading streak of discolored wood.

At this point in time, I was very much alone in my approach. I was already searching, in a kind of fantasy quest, for those with direct knowledge of pre-industrial practices that corresponded with what I was seeing in historic timber frames. I was particularly entranced by the carpentry work in my family's historic home in Picardie, which seemed so far from what I was witnessing at my construction job. On the other hand, *le trait de charpente* ("stereotomy" or "developed drawing" [5]) and *piquage au plomb* (the French plumbline scribe layout system) were still in widespread use. They were put into practice at my company's workshop by an old carpenter from the Ardèche region known as "the bungler." He wasn't a *compagnon*, and his accent and patois were so pronounced that I never managed to understand a word of his explanations. Another carpenter from the Ardèche was known only by his last name Bazelle because, as he told us, his first name was reserved for other situations. He was the

archetype of a site foreman: a big loudmouth but without malice, and on the job he was called "the raiser." The bungler and the raiser were the two central personalities of this carpentry company, which otherwise hired itinerants and apprentice workers.

That was the work at the jobsite. At the *compagnon* chapter-house where I was lodged, I remember indefatigable *compagnons* of whom we could ask technical questions regardless of the time of day or night, to learn more of our trade. But I also remember the brutality of certain journeymen who would hit young apprentices for the slightest infraction, real or imagined.

In France at that time, to my knowledge no carpenter (whether old or young) was practicing the craft in relationship with the forest and the natural world, as had been done for so many

centuries past. Both for my own curiosity and for my ethnology thesis (which I was preparing simultaneously to working as a carpenter), I began to search out those who might quench my thirst for know-how and connection to French architectural and craft heritage. I was able to meet two key people who would make a lasting impression on my approach: Paul Dubois, born in Muidorge (Oise, France, 1898-1992), who was part of a long line of country carpenters in Picardie, and who had never used a machine in his career; and Ivan (Jean) Urbiha, born at Gerovo (Croatia, 1915-2007). I am indebted to Ivan for having been the first to show me the use of the heavy Croation hewing axe called the *bradvil*, which left me astonished and appreciative. This tool, which he had brought to France from his native country, carried the name of its creator, a forge called Urh, in Čabar, Croatia. [6] Carried out on a dry (and therefore hardened) log, this

hewing demonstration must have been particularly difficult, but I was still ignorant of the significance of these subtleties.

Ivan was a retired logger who had come to France in 1937, bringing with him tools and techniques from his native region, Slavonia. Afterwards, he did me the honor of gifting his tools to me; I still cherish his *bradvil* (double-bevel axe), *stranak* (single-bevel axe with offset handle), and his log-dogs with perpendicular ends. A film by Jean-Dominique Lajoux of the CNRS (the French National Center for Scientific Research) documents the old tradition of Croatian foresters' *savoir-faire* that could have easily been lost with the death of Ivan Urbiha, but which is now preserved with astonishing vitality in the expert hands of young French carpenters who have learned to hew with the Yugoslavian *bradvil* axe. [7]

The fall of the Berlin wall allowed me to explore the countries of Eastern Europe, in the wake of the vast flow of new trade between Western Europe and the countries of the former Soviet bloc. In Romania, for example, certain rural regions had remained protected from the steam-rolling of the Soviet system. As such, Ceauşescu system-atization hadn't spread into the mountainous Carpathian region, and technological invasions hadn't been able to drain the peoples' reservoirs of ancestral know-how.

While traversing the Romanian countryside in 1991, I encountered a village called Vaideeni (in Oltania) populated entirely by wood artisans of the Rudari Roma ethnicity, who made a very diverse array of wooden instruments and tools and who worked only with hand tools. [8] In the village of Hobita (hometown of the famous sculptor Brancuşi), next to the roadway, I was entranced to see farmers hewing beams for their own house with axes. That experience spawned our first international hand-tool carpentry project, with the help of the ethnographer Titi Rusan and the Romanian folk museum Arta Lemnului. In Romania in May of 1992 over the course of 12 days, a team of Romanian carpenters built several projects using only hand tools, including an octagonal well of stacked-log construction in the local vernacular style. Concurrently, a French team (including notables Roland Doré, a carpenter from Picardie, and the *compagnon* Jean-Jacques Soulas "Bordelais l'Enfant du Progrès") demonstrated working with the *piquage au plomb* scribe technique, unknown to the Romanians. The French team had brought a scale model of a French-style hipped roof frame, featuring hip rafters cut with their backing angle and jack rafters joining the hip at compound angles. After looking it over, the Moldovan carpenters declared that if they had to work in that complex style, they'd be condemned to die of hunger! On the other hand, they showed an impressive dexterity with hand tools, including the famous *barda*. (See the book *Charpentiers au Travail*, under the direction of F. Calame, 1993 éditions À Die.)

"Man is a Tool-using Animal. Weak in himself, and of small stature. . . . Feeblest of bipeds! . . . Nevertheless he can use Tools; can devise Tools: with these the granite mountain melts into light dust before him; he kneads glowing iron, as if it were soft paste; seas are his smooth highway, winds and fire his unwearying steeds. Nowhere do you find him without Tools; without Tools he is nothing, with Tools he is all."

– Thomas Carlyle, *Sartor Resartus*

OPPOSITE: May 1992. Romania, Bucovina, Campulung Moldovenesc. A local carpenter using the broadaxe, the *barda*. The shape of this tool is quite similar to the German *breitbeil*.

RIGHT: Romania, Oltenia, Hobiţa. A local farmer hewing beside the road with his *barda* for the construction of his own house.

Photos: François Calame

In 2001, the project "Wood Culture in Europe" was launched by Nuria Sanz, with the support of the Council of Europe. This Europe-wide initiative enabled the development of diverse partnerships between nations concerned with their wooden architectural heritage. Though useful for fostering contacts and sharing perspectives, this program was similar to others of its type, plagued by the human tendency towards bureaucracy, and favoring theoretical and institutional perspectives rather than direct, physical exchanges of skills and know-how.

In 2002, we had the opportunity to organize the first *Charpentiers Sans Frontières* project in France, in which participants from eight countries came together to help preserve a beautiful fortified farm in the village of Beaumont in the Eure department of Normandy. Two objectives were pursued simultaneously: that of creating a social, cultural, and scientific experience focused on the carpentry trade and wooden architectural heritage; and that of working together over a short period of time to complete a carpentry project at a high level of craftsmanship, allowing for a real exchange of techniques and practices between carpenters from many nations. At this point in time, not a single carpenter in France had the skill to efficiently hew with a broadaxe. On the other hand, the art of *le trait de charpente* was widely practiced at a very high level, and was unanimously recognized as a specialty of French carpenters (a specialty they share, in fact, with their German counterparts).

From there, CSF continued its work in various countries. Ongoing collaboration with the UK's Carpenters Fellowship gave us much support, and the dynamic practices of the open-air museums in Great Britain, such as at Singleton, gave us inspiration. French companies specializing in the preservation of national historic monuments sometimes sent employees to participate in these exchanges, though not with the intention of expanding their range of work practices to include hand-tool work. These companies were not interested in questioning their own work practices – they used as little hand work as possible in order to maximize speed and profitability. As for carpenters from Eastern European countries (Poland and Romania), we knew them to be very competent with hand tools, but it proved difficult to attract them to CSF projects outside of (and even within) their own countries. The participants drawn to our projects have typically been scholars or architects, but not tradespeople, whose low socioeconomic status (and lack of English or French language skills) often means they are unable to get away from their day job. The same was true in Turkey: it was impossible to get the authentic Turkish hand-work artisans (for example, basket makers, ship builders, and pit sawyers whose expertise still flourished in 2001 but had already disappeared by 2008) to participate. Later, we encountered the same problem in China, where it was difficult to find professional tradespeople to participate (the only time CSF has been able to get a master Chinese carpenter to participate in a project in France was when I happened to discover that a Chinese businessman was renovating a château in Normandy using undocumented Chinese carpenters – they were willing participants!). During this same period, I also saw the last blacksmiths disappearing from villages around the world. Over the years we've been doing this CSF work, we've sometimes witnessed the sudden extinction of authentic ancestral know-how, even while there has been a growing aspiration within our modern society towards the revival of manual trades.

The *Compagnon* Guild organization has not been open to my proposals to collaborate; they thought our hand-tool focus was marginal compared to what they considered "real carpentry." It's important to note that my invitations to collaborate also fell on deaf ears of architects. Even today numerous architects, including those who specialize in historic monuments, have no interest in prioritizing the use of hand tools in historic carpentry restoration. This contrasts curiously with their approach to conservation of historic monuments built from stone. The craft of stone-cutting, which is considered the noblest of the building trades, has had no difficulty in preserving its attachment to hand-tool work, typically for hand-dressing the visible finished surfaces of stone blocks. Stone-cutting's similarity to the highly valued handcraft of classical sculpture has also helped it to retain use of hand tools. For wood, most often hidden in the obscurity of attics and under floors, hand-tool treatment has been digested by the processes of our techno-economic evolution.

Despite all that, Carpenters Without Borders has been organizing hand-tool carpentry projects with increasing frequency, sometimes in France and sometimes on other horizons. These projects always benefit from the priceless experiences and skills exchanged between friends from many nations.

As our work went on, Yves Lescroart, inspector general of historic monuments in France, took a great interest in the question of reviving traditional carpentry techniques. But it wasn't until the involvement of Régis Martin, chief architect of French historic monuments, that hand-tool carpentry was recognized as having a place on a jobsite of a French historic monument (i.e., a job of the highest level of importance to national heritage). This was the restoration of the Hautot-Mesnil Manor at Montreuil-en-Caux in the Seine-Maritime province in 2007. Many other historic monument projects have followed, all of which have benefited from the élan and the formidable reservoir of know-how offered by Carpenters Without Borders. Since 2002 – not counting the exploratory project in Romania in 1992 – 14 other CSF projects have taken place around the world, bringing craftspeople together around

Luo Yin Jin, a Chinese carpenter, ethnic minority Buyi, at *Charpentiers Sans Frontières* workshop in Guizhou area in August 2015. The task was to build a traditional Chinese timber-framed building. We worked in partnership with Ruan Yisan Heritage Foundation.

Photo: François Calame

a project where they can practice their art. Often working with historical architecture, the theme of the project might also be social or humanitarian. For example, in 2015, CSF member Mourad Manesse initiated a CSF project to build a timber-framed legal aid center for refugees seeking asylum in the unofficial refugee camp in Calais, France, infamously known as the "Jungle."

Participants come from all over the world in the spirit of exchange, learning, and friendship. Warm and long-term relationships have been made with North American carpenters and experts since 2017. These friends have refreshed the perspectives of us carpenters from old Europe with their enthusiasm, generosity, and their innovative technical intel-ligence. In Sedgwick, Maine in 2019, in the welcoming arms of the *Mortise & Tenon* family, we all had the strong feeling that together, we could move mountains.

The heritage of our crafts, the renewed relationship to wood and to the skills that allow us to act with and for wood, are changing our broader relationship to matter and the material world. The creative energy of Carpenters Without Borders clearly shows that cultural heritage isn't preserved – it is transmitted.

LEFT: Heinrich Groff. Detail from *Silver mine of La Croix-aux-Mines, Lorraine,* fol.3r. (1530).

OPPOSITE: Workshop at Château de Gaillon, Eure, Normandy in 2013. Forty carpenters from France, UK, Norway, Germany, Canada, USA, Belgium, and Iceland worked together to restore the roof of the Tour de la Sirène. The oak trees came from the castle yard and were felled by axes the winter before the work. The leader of the work was Florian Carpentier.

Photo: François Calame

ENDNOTES

1. The *Compagnons du Devoir*, or "Companions of Duty," is an ancient trades guild dating back to around 1000 A.D. Their history and evolution is a complex subject. Still active today, the *compagnonnage* has adapted to modern methods and technology while also retaining a fair amount of traditional know-how and ritual. There is very little English-language information about the *Compagnons*; for more historical information, see *The Artisans and Guilds of France* by François Icher.

2. The term *moise* first appears in 1631 under the definition : "a beam pit-sawn in half." (Père Phil. Monet, *Abrégé du parallèle des langues françaises et latine*).

3. Each *compagnon*, upon completing their apprenticeship and journeyman training, is received as a full Companion in a special ceremony at which s/he is given a special name, reflecting his or her geographical origins and personality.

4. The French term for king post truss, *ferme latine*, dates back to the trusses conceived by the Roman architect Vitruvius, which used basic principles of triangulation and were well known across France since Roman times.

5. *Le trait de charpente* is an ancient, extremely refined technique of geometric drafting which enables the practitioner to solve enormously complex geometrical problems and then transfer them from two-dimensional drawings to three-dimensional material. Virtually unknown in North America, this technique is sometimes called "stereotomy," "descriptive geometry," or "developed drawing." *Le trait* is one of the core technical skills of French carpentry, and in particular has been protected, refined, and transmitted through the *Compagnon* guild system for the last thousand years. It was recognized as Intangible Cultural Heritage by UNESCO in 2009 based on an application made by François Calame.

6. The Urh family forge still exists at Čabar, in the mountains near the border with Slovenia.

7. Among those adept with the *bradvil*, I'll mention Léonard Rousseau, Paul Zahnd, and Julien Hubin.

8. The Rudari people of Oltenia in Romania are known in other Balkan countries as Boyash people. Their artisanal woodcraft is on track to disappear, and today is limited to spoon carving and bobbin fabrication for homespun wool.

Essay translated by Will Gusakov.

CHAPTER I
A New Work

"A society of simple tools that allows men to achieve purposes with energy fully under their own control is now difficult to imagine. Our imaginations have been industrially deformed to conceive only what can be molded into an engineered system of social habits that fit the logic of large-scale production. . . . We have all grown up as children of our time, and therefore it is extremely difficult to envisage a postindustrial yet human type of 'work.'"

Ivan Illich — *Tools for Conviviality*

On March 10th, 2019, timber framer Will Lisak sent me a text message:

"François has been asking us if we'd have any interest in hosting a CSF project in the US, but we don't have a project. Can you think of any person or institution that needs some work done?"

I couldn't believe what I was reading. How amazing that these folks were coming to my country! It would be worth a road trip just to watch them work. As the conversation developed, I brought up the small blacksmith and wood shed projects that Mike and I had in our minds as an idea, but mentioned it only as a side comment. I assumed it would lead nowhere, but Will brought our ideas to the team, and before I knew it, a CSF project at our place became a viable option.

After a couple weeks of discussion, François and the rest of the crew responded with a confirmed interest in my informal, offhand proposal. I was dumbfounded. It sent my mind reeling: What kind of preparation would be involved? What would feeding and housing more than 40 people at our place for more than a week look like? What would this mean for our entire year's schedule? Could we even pull off such a thing? At that point, my wife, Julia, and I had already resolved to keep our 2019 summer schedule light, because of pushing hard the several summers prior. But we realized immediately that we simply could not resist such an offer.

To begin the planning process, I was introduced to Will Gusakov and Hank Silver, the two US team leaders on this project. Will G. and I talked on the phone and exchanged many emails to work out the details of what such a frame would look like. After months of serious discussion, planning, and research, the question that I kept coming back to was, "When is this official?" Before I purchased granite for the foundation or logs for the frame, I had to be sure that this event would pan out. There were so many people involved and so many parts to fit together that it took some time. But when the French team forwarded their flight confirmation to my inbox, I knew this was happening. I called the quarry and ordered the granite blocks that day.

"What is wanted is a larger interest in the [carpentry] craft, a fuller knowledge of the part it has fulfilled in the communal life of past days, a grasp of the ideals and principles that controlled the efforts of the men who made it, and a firm belief that what men have done in the past a man may do to-day.

"This may involve an alternate change over from the spirit of the modern to the antique. The temper of the present day rightly insists that modern comforts shall be introduced into old-world houses. This, with skill, can be done without altering their original character, and frequently tests the ability of the local craftsman."

– Walter Rose, *The Village Carpenter*

Will Gusakov and François Calame on the jobsite in Sedgwick, Maine.

BENT 3 - OPEN BELOW TIE BEAM

3/8

1/4" = 1'

PEAK DETAIL
IN FIELD:

OVERALL RUN
14' 1 11/16"

10' 8 3/16" to spline

LOG RAFTER

2 1/4

2' 10"

5' 1"

6" natural,
scribe m

8' 5"

8'

12"

2"

SEE DETAIL
ON OTHER
SHEET

8 x 10

3' 6"

5 natural,
scribe m

5'

8 x 8

11' 4"

1' 2" (not to)

WALL A

WALL B

1'

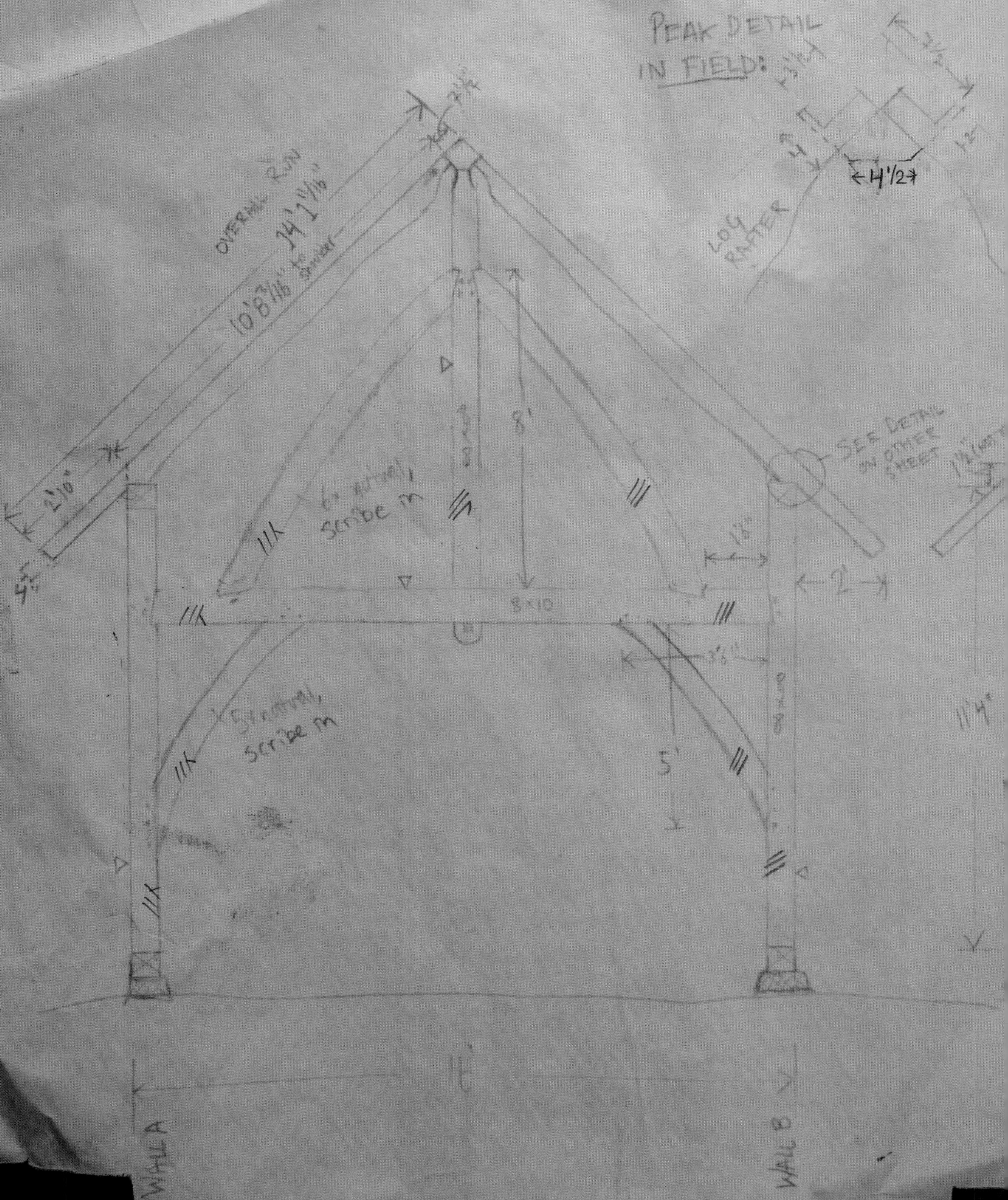

A Conversation with the Frame's Designer, Will Gusakov of Goosewing Timberworks

WG: There were a lot of different factors. The first logistical considerations were coming up with a design that would be achievable in a week-long project for Carpenters Without Borders. Secondly, we looked at your needs for *Mortise & Tenon*. Through our conversations, I got a sense of the sort of structure were you envisioning, and I was delighted to discover you were interested in a classic New England-style frame. I had actually been hoping that we could do a typical American barn frame for this project because that would make a nice project for Europeans to work on so they could be related to the local place and the vernacular architecture.

Those were the overall guiding considerations, and we were all on the same page. I worked on a design that incorporated a lot of classic northern New England timber-frame typology. But I also added pieces that would lend themselves well to European or French scribe techniques – that's a bit of a departure from the New England style but not a vast one.

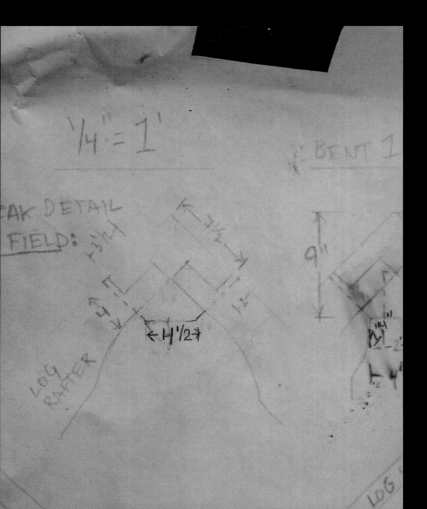

WG: The New England style was descended from British framing types and arrangements. This differs from Hudson Valley or Pennsylvania frames, which generally descended from German and Dutch framing traditions, but there are intersections and crossovers between timber-framing traditions all the way back to Europe, where most US timber frame styles came from. A classic New England barn frame of the 19th century is organized by bents, has continuous tie beams and wall plates, with tie beams dropped below the wall plate level to give a little bit of a knee wall upstairs – that was something of a new-world arrangement.

The one-piece pentagonal ridge with common rafters is also a classic feature of 19th-century northern New England framing, too. In southern coastal New England and in Dutch framing you'll find principal rafters and common purlins, but in northern New England there are a lot of common-rafter roofs.

JK: What is the benefit of a pentagonal ridge?

WG: The point of the five-sided ridge beam is to have 90° bearing within the rafter planes, meaning the top two surfaces of the ridge are within the roof plane, and the two side surfaces are square to the roof plane. The bottom is just whatever angle you're left with. So the point is to normalize that bearing to make the joinery easier to lay out and cut on the ridge. For roof pitches other than 12/12 [rise in inches/12" run], this makes a noticeable difference – it's really nice to deal with squareness on that corner.

JK: When and where in history was the five-sided ridge beam common?

WG: I can't answer that definitively, but I do know they were used in New England from the late 1700s onwards and mostly disappeared from use in the middle of the 19th century. They became rarer during that time because they require more work. As timber framing was becoming pared-down and economized on its way to becoming stick framing, things like five-sided ridges with all of the mortise-and-tenon joints got nixed. Often, late-19th-century timber frames' rafters just had a plumb cut and a couple nails between them.

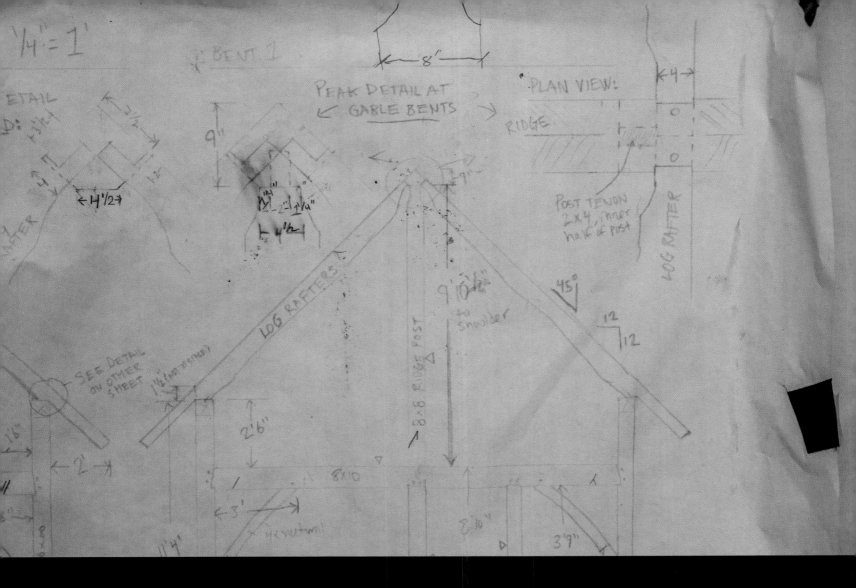

JK: What is the function of the fifth side – the flat on the bottom? Why is that there?

WG: There's not really a function, per se. I think it's mostly aesthetic, though in this project we had ridge posts and bracing to support the ridge. Adding posts is not unheard of, but it is less common than a ridge supported only by rafters, which in turn are supported by the plates. That means that, in those roof systems, the tie joints of the tie beams are what's holding the roof ridge up. That's the typical construction of outbuildings, but I like to add ridge posts because it takes away all the rafter thrust at the walls and makes the building a lot more rugged and resilient over time. So in our case, we needed flat spots at least at the joints with braces and posts. But there are many frames without ridge posts that also have the flat on the bottom, so I think it's just aesthetic, honestly.

In reality, it would just be funny to have a bottom arris extend down into the room, especially with a typical New England barn pitch of 9 or 9-1/2. The lower the pitch, the more trapezoidal the ridge gets, and if you didn't have a flat bottom, that arris would be 12" or 14" deep – a really acute angle at the bottom. So part of it is just practical as well – you have to chop it off somewhere, so I guess they just snapped a line and hewed it.

JK: How old is the common-rafter roof system? Did it come after the principal-rafter, common-purlin system?

WG: Lots of medieval roof framing in Europe is common rafter, but it's tricky to talk this way because in reality it's not that there are only two systems. It's easy to divide them into princi-

pal rafter, common purlins, and common rafter, but it's not that simple because often there are layers of framing that we might call rafters that are not within the roof plane. This is a classical French way of doing it. They have their own name for it in French, but we would call them principal rafters. Then on top of those there are purlins that run along the length of the building including the ridge. Then, on top of those are the common rafters. That's traditional in a lot of medieval cathedrals. Larger buildings were built like that, so using common rafters has been around for thousands of years.

WG: The criterion for the design of the frame from the beginning was that it would be a physical reflection of our rendezvous, as well as an educational exposure to the different traditions that we brought with us.

The frame we made is essentially a typical 1840 or 1850 New England barn frame. It's laid out with the American-invented layout system called square-rule. "Square" refers to the framing square, not square as in the shape. This system represents the American timber-framing knowledge and tradition. Then we worked in some curvy timbers that were laid out with the French *piquage* scribe method. This incorporated the tradition of the French, and to an extent the British as well. Generally speaking, scribing is the European way of conceptualizing, organizing, and laying out timber for building.

So including the naturally curved braces and the struts in bent three allowed us to have an exchange of teaching in which the Americans taught the Europeans square-rule, but then at one point during the week we switched, and the French crew taught their version of *piquage* for laying out the braces and the struts.

JK: How does the white pine that was commonly used for framing in northern New England affect the frame's design or joinery?

WG: Hugely. And not just what species but what quality – the timber's length, straightness, and freedom from knots. A lot of the innovations, styles, and typologies that came to be

known as distinctly North American developed thanks to the timber. That's largely because of the quality that was available. Softwoods in general grow with less branching than hardwoods, so using softwoods allows for pretty consistent, straight timber, and having regular timbers led to the development of this square-rule layout system.

You can use square-rule to join curvy or funky pieces of timber, but it's not the most efficient system for that. It is efficient at joining regular timbers. The beautiful, straight softwood forests in the eastern US were harvested since Europeans settled here. Around 1800, the square-rule system developed in response to the availability of this straight timber.

In terms of species preference, eastern white pine was preferred for framing. Certainly other softwoods were and are used: hemlock, spruce, tamarack. But pine is great because it's very stable, which is especially important because timber framing is done while the wood is still wet. It is green woodworking, and if timbers don't warp or twist or shrink all that much, that's valuable.

Usually the size of a beam or a post – what we call the timber "section" – isn't governed by the engineering loads on that timber. The section of a timber is usually governed by how much space there needs to be to accept the joinery coming in. That being the case, an 8" x 8" post has some ridiculous amount of strength in compression just standing up in a building – much more than is needed – but it's sized to hold the joinery shared with the other timbers in the frame. White pine is plenty strong in the type of sections that are used in timber framing.

Carpenters in southern New England framed with oak as well, right alongside pine

frames, but I don't notice drastic differences in timber sections. A typical post size is 8" x 8" whether it's oak or pine. I'm sure it has to do with traditions and conventions, but also that's just a good size to accept lots of 2" mortise-and-tenon joints coming in.

JK: How do traditional standards, dimensions, and methods compare to modern methods of framing?

WG: You'd have to define what you mean by modern framing, because if you mean the state-of-the-art electric tools in a shop, the most modern these days are multi-million-dollar Hundegger CNC timber cutting machines that you can load an AutoCAD frame plan into and feed in raw timber, and it spits out finished timbers that are ready to raise. Predictably, that's the way more people are going. It's unfortunate.

That's of course the extreme, but in a typical smaller shop, one big difference from traditional practice is that most places depend on building codes and oversight, and so the design needs to be approved by a structural engineer. That's very different from earlier times, in which the framer was responsible for the integrity of the frame and there wasn't a certified professional that had his or her liability on the line. Because not a lot of today's engineers understand timber framing well, many modern timber framing designs have shifted based on pressure to use elements that these engineers are comfortable staking their professional liability on – that is why folks are adding steel plates and bolts or hidden steel fasteners. It also explains the oversizing of timber sections and the overly conservative spacing of rafters and joists.

Even if a design element has been proven historically, the engineers want it to work in their

computer models. They have huge factors of safety, and at least on paper, they're upping the strength of buildings. There's a funny thing in the field of timber frame restoration – most of us have buildings that we've known or taken down or studied that engineers will put into their software, and the buildings fall down in the computer model even though they've been standing neglected for 200 years. Even the ones that have had a bad roof and a leak and some rot here and there for 150 years are still doing fine. But you put them in the engineer's model and they fall down right away. That shows that the models are not really so real-world accurate. The question about what's changed in the last 200 years is a big one.

JK: I heard you say that because this CSF frame is handmade, you wanted to draw the plans by by hand. Could you elaborate on that? What was the value in your mind in drawing this by hand?

WG: I draw by hand all the time for my own shop drawings and even for simple projects when communicating with the client or other contractors. I have refused to spend the time in front of a computer learning SketchUp or any of the other modeling software programs – to my own professional detriment, no doubt, but surely to my own personal benefit.

Hank Silver, who co-led the project, is fluent in using SketchUp and offered to render everything in the software. It would have been a lot easier for me, and in some ways, easier to make changes after the drawing was complete, but because I love drawing by hand, and because I was inspired by this being an all-hand-tool project, I felt like the plans should be hand-drawn as well.

We actually changed a relatively major part of the design going from a square ridge with rafters that join into it with bird's-mouths, to a five-sided ridge and rafters with tenons one week before the project, and I spent several hours at the drafting table erasing, redrawing, and adding lots of detail views that I wouldn't normally draw for my own shop drawings. Because we were going to be communicating among nearly 40 framers of different nationalities, the detailed drawings really helped. That was a ton of fun actually. I loved it.

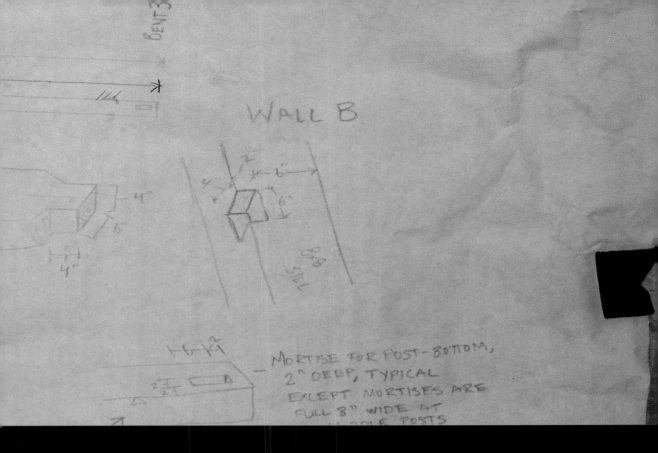

Within the image area, handwritten notes: BENT 3, WALL B, SILL 8×8, MORTISE FOR POST—BOTTOM, 2" DEEP, TYPICAL EXCEPT MORTISES ARE FULL 8" WIDE AT MIDDLE POSTS

JK: Were there any other interesting historic features that you wanted to make sure were incorporated into this design?

WG: It was typical for 19th-century New England framing to have log joists and log rafters in which just one plane was hewn flat, and the rest of it was left in the round. It was typical for attics and cellars to have log rafters and joists, because it's a time-saving thing when you're hewing your timber from logs. If you don't actually need the other surfaces of the timber to be squared, you can save an awful lot of time and effort by only hewing one surface flat. It makes cutting the joinery a little bit more challenging, but there are simple ways to get around that.

JK: What was the biggest takeaway you got from this project?

WG: During the project, we were all talking amongst ourselves, realizing that if one were to analyze what we were doing economically, everybody got a really bad deal. The carpenters donated thousands and thousands of dollars of work and travel, and if you counted the *M&T* team's

hustle and labor on top of the expenses, it probably cost more than if it were purchased from a professional company. So, economically speaking, everybody lost out. But it was so great because everyone came away beaming and feeling like they just had the greatest week-and-a-half of their lives. And we made a really beautiful structure. It's so beautiful to see how economics don't reflect everything.

Coming away from this experience, I've been thinking that if my colleague, Zakari LeBlanc, and I have a little bit of downtime, we'd build an all-hand-tool small spec frame. I am anxious to design something I *want* to design and to document that process. I'm inspired to make a small frame with hand tools because of what we did with CSF. It's got me thinking lately that I should push to do more of the type of work I *want* to do.

SHOWING THE WORLD THAT ANOTHER WORK IS POSSIBLE

From August 22nd to 31st, 2019, my wife and I hosted and fed a crew of more than 40 people as they hand-hewed, joined, and raised a 16' x 25' blacksmith shop for our publication, *Mortise & Tenon Magazine*. The construction took place over eight days and the frame was raised in one half day. This build was an inspiring demonstration of understanding and skill, and moreover, that another work is possible: Instead of working in isolation, dependent on machinery and manufactured building materials, we can claim our humanity by learning to use simple tools to create structures of lasting beauty. We can pick up a rusty axe that's already had two centuries of use, give it a fresh edge, and set it to work to accomplish incredible things. And because this way of building is an investment in labor rather than expensive machinery, it is something that anyone can do.

It's not necessary to fly to another country or host 40 carpenters to do this. With nothing more than an axe, a chisel, and a saw, you can learn to shape your own environment. Average folks throughout history did this kind of thing themselves – every farm had an axe or two for such projects. Even though professional carpenters have been around a long time, in the pre-industrial mindset, hewing logs into timbers was simply an unremarkable thing to do. It was the sort of job you hired local kids to do with you.

The people I know building their lives with their own two hands succeed by simplifying their obligations and doing things for themselves. It's amazing how much time and opportunity open up when we minimize the amount of stuff that we have to maintain and reduce the "necessary" expenses in our lives. Bill Coperthwaite built beautiful, simple yurts on his property in rural Maine and filled them with handmade things even though he "never had much money," and ended up "living all of his life well below what our government calls the poverty line." This became possible for Bill because he made a "consistent choice of time over money" throughout his 55 years in his "experiment in living." [1] He succeeded because he refused to get sucked into the rat race.

Outward Bound founder Kurt Hahn's philosophical leitmotif, "*Plus est en Vous* – There is more in you than you think," has been an inspiration to many. The benefits of a direct and personal relationship to your own work cannot be bought, and embracing the sweat and challenge of this work is worth everything we put into it. It is only through hard work that we can discover our potential.

The Carpenters Without Borders team has also shown us that physical work is even more fulfilling when done with friends and family. There's a lot of beautiful work to be done at a project like this that has little to do with an axe edge or timber. Sure, there's hewing and hauling, but there's also cooking, and feasting, and laughing, and good stories to tell. And this camaraderie forges friendships through an experience that is rarely seen today. CSF models the power of joyful hand work. Through their efforts, we've seen not only that many hands make light work (which is very true!), but that the bonds built through sharing labor and sweating

side-by-side prove to be the most rich and lasting. We need this new vision for our work in this world.

My sister-in-law recently got glasses. She had been navigating her daily routines with fuzzy vision for years without knowing any different, but when she set those frames to her eyes for the first time she realized just how nearsighted she was. "I had no idea there were small branches on those trees," she marveled. Suddenly, with a newly cleared vision, her daily experience changed radically. The world for her is no longer a series of blurry shapes – now there is depth, contour, and definition.

Even if we as children were once able to behold the beauty and richness of life, too many of us eventually lose the vision. Whether it is because of an apathy born out of affluence, the ever-increasing number of technological devices cluttering our lives, or something else entirely, our senses can dull, making us a little more numb to the world around us. And if the sweetness of life becomes much too obscured, we ultimately lose heart and purpose. Human beings were designed to work – it is written in our blood. Through the engaged use of our bodies, we can discover a connection with the world around us that we didn't even know was possible. We have been made for this.

"Work is a good thing for man – a good thing for his humanity – because through work man *not only transforms nature*, adapting it to his own needs, but he also *achieves fulfilment* as a human being..."

- John Paul II, *Laborem Exercens*

CHAPTER 2

Rooted in Nature

"The cultivation and expansion of needs is the antithesis of wisdom. It is also the antithesis of freedom and peace. Every increase of needs tends to increase one's dependence on outside forces over which one cannot have control. . . . Ever-bigger machines, entailing ever-bigger concentrations of economic power and exerting ever-greater violence against the environment, do not represent progress: they are a denial of wisdom. Wisdom demands a new orientation of science and technology towards the organic, the gentle, the non-violent, the elegant and beautiful."

E.F. Schumacher — *Small is Beautiful*

THE FRAME'S FOUNDATION

Granite has been quarried from Deer Isle, Maine since the 1860s, and because of its quality, has found its way into buildings and monuments across the country. I chose a locally sourced granite-on-grade foundation system after consulting with stone mason Dennis Carter of Deer Isle. Dennis hand-split and stacked the entire foundation for the Deer Isle Hostel, which he and his wife, Anneli, run. He hand-hewed, salvaged, and milled the timbers of the frame, which was based on several 17th-century Massachusetts houses he examined. He milled most of the boards from local trees himself. He handplaned just about every floor and wall board, made his own windows, and mixed his own paint. Dennis is exactly the kind of guy you want to talk to when you're thinking about putting up a handmade building.

In my conversations with him, Dennis explained that many of the foundations he's built are based on those he observed in Sweden. The system is simple: The frame sills rest on large boulders set on grade. In order to avoid pooled water contacting the sills, a smaller stone is placed between the boulder and sill. Since his visit to Sweden, Dennis has done this himself many times with granite blocks quarried in Deer Isle by Francis Cormier, a man whose knowledge and expertise in all things granite are evident.

Cormier delivered the 16" x 16" x 16" blocks mid-June, just in time for our six woodworking workshop students to give us a hand setting them. The *M&T* workshop model is that of a work exchange – the students give us two days of labor helping with various projects, and we give them three days of in-the-shop instruction. No money

"The Barn-Elm"
Robert P.T. Coffin

There has not been the sound of a hoof
For forty years under this roof,
Not a solitary sound of a cud
Turning red clover into red blood.

No hens have made gilt fogs in the litter
Scratching up corns with the golden glitter,
No little pigs for forty years now
Have pressed the keyboard along a sow.

No hay upstairs in umber mows,
Rust has reddened harrows and plows,
The barn houses only waifs and thieves,
Mice, silky swallows under the eaves.

Yet life was here once beautifully,
And if you doubt it, there is the tree,
A tree like a universe, tall as pride,
Covers the barn, white side to side.

No tree could reach such beauty and size
Without a century of sunflower eyes,
The hoofed, the cleft, the three-toed feet,
Hay falling from heaven for beasts to eat.

A hundred horses, a thousand hens
Escaped the stalls, escaped the pens,
Escaped the fact that they must die,
Rose in green arches on the sky.

Now here they are, cascading branches,
Laces of twigs by avalanches,
Singing hens turned to singing boughs,
An elm tree built of horses and cows.

changes hands, and the arrangement is a win-win. Cameron, Tino, Matija, Mare, Hugo, Ash, Mike, and I will always remember the time we spent working side-by-side, digging the holes to level the blocks. This was especially memorable for Tino, who discovered a massive boulder just beneath the surface of the location of the center block. We reached out to Dennis for advice and borrowed the tools for the job: the hammer drill, feathers and wedges, and sledgehammers. After considerable grunting, sweating, and beating, we removed enough of the rock that our block could sit level in the hole. We are grateful to every one of our students for their help with that foundation – the blocks were set in one good day's work.

Conventional building practice in colder climates avoids using blocks on grade as a foundation because of potential issues with frost heaving. To prevent this from happening, modern builders dig into the ground below the frost line (4' here in Maine) and pour concrete. I was not keen on the idea of concrete and started looking into options that had historic precedent. It turns out that folks for a long time have put their barns and outbuildings on a foundation of stacked fieldstone right on grade. The reason this works is the frame's construction method. When a frame is joined and pegged, there is no way that the building will fall apart if or when the blocks move at seasonal transitions. It's a flexible system. Especially if there is nothing rigidly installed, such as plaster or plumbing, it is unlikely to cause headaches in the long run. Dennis showed us how easy it is to jack the sill to swap out the top stone for a different size if needed. It's a straightforward and quick adjustment.

SOURCING THE LOGS

Looking over the timber list I got from Will Gusakov, I contemplated (and explored) several avenues to try to secure the logs we needed for the frame, including conventional timber-harvesting operations. From the beginning, my ideal choice was to work with horse logger, timber framer, and organic farmer Jon Ellsworth.

Jon logs his carefully managed 140-acre woodlot in Brooklin, Maine with his sturdy Suffolk Punch horses, Jay and Jackson. His lot is next to my former workshop, and I often remember hearing the confident trot of Jon's team coming up the road to head out into the woods as I worked away at my bench. It is inspiring to see these horses in their element, eager to work. Jay and Jackson are creatures of immense beauty, and seeing such a gentle soul as Jon collaborate with the two of them to manage and husband the forest is a heartening thing.

To meet our deadline, Jon's services would be required during July and August – his busiest months on the farm. I knew this was a lot to ask of him, and so I was not surprised when his initial response was that he'd love to, but there was no way he could fit it in. He informed me that he'd promised his wife, Jennifer, that he would not take on any timber-frame projects that summer so they could focus on the farm. He sounded disappointed, but resolute – it just wasn't possible.

Until he called me back the next day. "Hey Joshua. I've got an idea…"

After talking it over with Jennifer, he was trying hard to find a way to be involved with the project, and within a week or two, Jon was able to shuffle his schedule around enough to find time to log the entire frame during the peak of summer madness on the farm. I am still stunned and grateful for his and Jennifer's willingness to take this on. It means so much to have the logs from their beautifully managed forest now standing as a building on our property.

Jon's philosophy of forest management is rooted in his deep respect for the natural world. For nearly 30 years, he has managed this mixed-species woodland at his farm in Brooklin, Maine. From his years involved with Hancock County's Low-Impact Forestry group, Jon learned sustainable practices that honor both the dignity of the forest and respectful human uses. Jon's desire is to cultivate tall, straight trees by selective cutting and hauling with his horses. With this low-impact approach, he ensures that the canopy overhead is never opened too much, which encourages the next tree that fills the space to grow tall and straight, reaching for the canopy without putting on too many limbs. He has often seen the reverse happen in clear-cut forests – trees that spring up after clearing grow full of limbs, because they are never challenged to stretch upward for sunlight. This makes knotty and undesirable lumber.

Because he sees his role as that of a steward, Jon's management practices stem from a long-term vision for these woods. His aim is that through respectful working of the land, every year the forest will be healthier, more diverse, and even more beautiful than the year before. He strives for a harmonious balance between the forest as a wilderness and the forest as a resource. Jon has developed a woodlot that is both productive in harvest and beautiful in its wildness.

Jon waited to begin the logging until mid-July in order to ensure that the logs would be as green as possible when the crew arrived at the end of August. He told me that he was amused to hear Will G. and Hank request the logs to be so freshly felled because, as a timber framer himself, he often has to quell his clients' concerns that the frames aren't dry enough. But timber framers have long known the secret that when it comes to logs, the wetter, the better.

Working carefully in the woods requires an understanding of the forest community

—

not just where to travel but how and why.

Some types of logging equipment are more damaging than others; the conditions of the forest floor — whether it's wet, dry, steep, or flat — are very important. Dragging logs with a wheeled logging arch makes the work easier, which means the logger can work the horses longer with less stress. When a forwarder, with its flotation tires and fully supported load, is kept from disturbing soil in those heavily traveled areas, it can save time and soil and preserve more of the ecosystem.

Timing, too, is important. Although dragging logs in September's dry days might disturb a little soil, the ground is soon covered again by the falling leaves. Frozen ground is rather impervious, and even a little snow will make any skidding much easier on the draft animals. But dragging in early spring just after ice-out makes a muddy mess. Some forest management goals prescribe limited soil disturbance, but there is no need to use specialized equipment, dedicated time, and fuel if one can integrate the equipment already in use.

Knowing which trees to cut and which to leave is akin to pruning apple trees successfully. Done well, the forest will increase in health and productivity. Done poorly, the value decreases with every harvest.

Learning to communicate with horses through hands, lines, and bit is best done before entering the woods, but every horse is different and methods must be adapted to each horse.

And there is much to know about felling a tree. Specific skills for axes or chainsaws will get the work done efficiently and safely. Knowing which direction to send the tree will save time and energy and other trees. Of course, one must know how to send the tree in the desired direction, too. Plunging the tip of the saw through the trunk and lining up with a cut from the other side is a skill the chainsaw operator needs to develop. Wedging the back cut to support the tree and push it in the desired direction will keep you alive. Skill with saw, peavey, and chain comes with time in the woods.

As with any work worth doing, developing and continually honing the skills required will always lead to better results. Work in the woods demands that we do it well. Indeed, our lives depend on it.

JASON BREEN, HORSE LOGGER, *USA*

Besides Jon's logs, the red pine rafters and second-floor joists were sourced in the woods below my woodshop. Mike and I spent several days before the carpenters arrived felling, limbing, and debarking these pines. The debarking process was relatively straightforward with my antique bark spud. Mike had another, modern version that seemed to be too sharp and had the wrong edge geometry – he was fighting pretty hard to be able to get sheets of bark to roll off. I'm no bark spud connoisseur, but there was a radical difference in performance between the two otherwise-identical tools. The relationship between intelligent tool design, quality natural materials, and the artisan's skill seemed to be the heartbeat of this entire project. When one of those is lacking, the work suffers. But when all three are present, work is an immense pleasure.

THE PROJECT BEGINS:
WEDNESDAY, AUGUST 21ST

During the course of negotiating the project timeline with everyone involved, we determined that the best time for this build would be the last week of August. Will Lisak, Loïc Desmonts, and Hank Silver arrived a few days before the rest of the team to designate logs for specific timbers, create over a dozen hewing stations, and organize tools. Mike and I (with help from several others) constructed a temporary outdoor kitchen, turned my woodshop into a dining room, got the two massive rental houses cleaned and set up with bedding, and executed an unending number of miscellaneous to-do items.

The site prep was facilitated by my neighbor's Massey Ferguson tractor. Once the logs were labeled on their end grain with lumber crayon, Will used the tractor to haul them down to the hewing stations. The stations were scattered down into the wooded area that Mike and I cleared for the rafters only days before. Once we opened that space, a beautiful worksite emerged, sparkling with filtered light through the forest canopy but shielded from the brunt of the summer sun. The magic of that forest setting inspired Loïc, Will, and Hank to make the most of the space for the construction process, by spreading the site into the trees. This proved to be a good call, because throughout the week of the project, I heard many remarks from the carpenters and the visiting public about the tranquility of the worksite. There is something magical about the direct connection between the craftsperson and the forest.

It is exactly the same magic I felt when walking Jon's woodlot as we discussed the project initially. To look at the finished frame and remember the trees as they stood is a vivid reminder that the forest is where this all begins. On one occasion, as Jon was leading me through acres and acres of woods, he pointed to individual stumps and made comments such as, "See that one right there? That's the corner post of so-and-so's barn." This kind of relationship with the woods is markedly different than anything I'd experienced previously. I knew that bringing together a team of people who share that same sensitive spirit would make this project unique.

As a way of celebrating the underappreciated parts of the forest's wild beauty, the braces for this frame were formed from curvy hardwoods – maple, wild cherry, red oak, and birch with dramatic arches. These days, this is the kind of wood that rarely finds a resting place anywhere other than the woodstove. But this stuff wasn't always ignored. In fact, artisans of all stripes (especially shipwrights, chairmakers, and carpenters) sought long and hard for all sorts of curves in nature. Because these craftsmen knew that lumber is dramatically stronger when the grain continues along the whole length, they went to great pains to select the natural curves that matched the final desired shape.

Although timber-framing work obliges Jon to cut exemplary trees from his lot, he says there are some that he'll never touch – "They'll die in those woods," he says. These standards are too beautiful, too majestic to be made into boards or beams. There are some foresters out there who think it is those great ones that set the bar for the rest of the trees, and when you remove them, the bar is lowered. Jon was taught, "When you take the best, your best gets worse."

Jon is a true steward, and his deep understanding of the interdependence of humanity and nature is also obvious in his farm work. Raising greens and vegetables is a discipline dependent on nature in the most obvious of ways. We can protect crops with row cover or we can insulate them in green houses, but no matter how sophisticated we make our farming, it will always be an endeavor indebted to the generosity of nature. Even the most controlled industrial farms invest in insurance against crop failure – "Acts of God," we acknowledge.

Along with the raw materials for the frame, there was also a tremendous amount of food required to fuel this hungry crew over the duration of the build, and a lot of sweat was produced to bring it from the soil. Almost everything we ate during the week was raised or grown within 15 minutes of the worksite. I cannot help wondering at the bounty of the fields providing the power for humans to build shelter from the bounty of the forest. The sun that produced that arugula is the same sun that nourished the trees. The rocky soil that grew those carrots also held the roots of the pines and tamaracks that Jon felled for us.

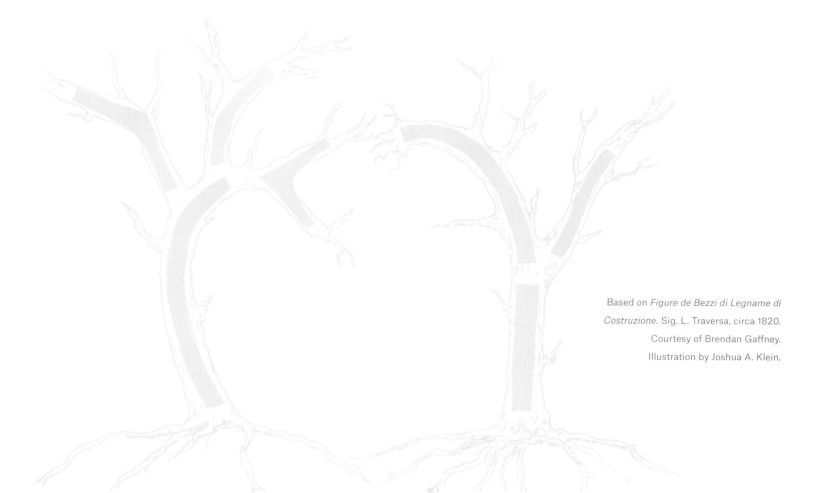

Based on *Figure de Bezzi di Legname di Costruzione*. Sig. L. Traversa, circa 1820. Courtesy of Brendan Gaffney. Illustration by Joshua A. Klein.

Let me tell you about how I have learned to talk to wood.

Before I fell a tree in the forest, I talk with him for a while to ask permission to fell him. I tell him why I want to do this and what I plan to make out of him. "Meet you soon," I say.

After felling the tree, the hewing begins. This is a process full of conversation. The tree at first is hiding under the bark and sleeps. He is scared at first, but I say "Hello," to him and "it's me again," and I remind him what I plan to make out of him. When I hew, I often meet branches. In my thinking, these branches are the eyes of a tree. When there are two branches near each other, I see them as two eyes. When I come to a branch, it is as if I open an eye. I try to hew the branch smooth – if I succeed, then the eye is smiling. If a chip breaks out, it's a crying eye. This is like our lives, in which there are smiles and tears along the way.

When I cut the log to length at a whorl of branches, it's more difficult to cut, but the reward is that you see a sun on the edge of the log – it is a joy shared between the log and the artisan.

When I mark and cut the joints into the log, he is again scared and thinks, "After this, what happens next?" But if the joint is successful, fitting perfect and tight, the timber meets another piece of wood and they are friends – they hold tight to each other and don't let go. It is the same as we do when life is scary. It's comforting to hold someone's hand tight – we feel safe and brave.

And so this is why I talk to wood. We are those masters who give a second life to a tree, who has grown for a century in the forest. We humans will never have the same fortune in our lives.

Friends, this work is an honor, trust, and responsibility.

ANDRES UUS, *ESTONIA*

It was important to us that we used fresh, local ingredients for the meals we shared, and the labor of many talented area producers and harvesters made this possible – from Julia's father, Scott, who has been tending an immensely productive family garden for many years; to Phil and Heather at Quill's End Farm, a grass-based farm and micro-dairy focused on healthy, regenerative stewardship of the land and the animals raised on it; to Jon and Jennifer, who (besides managing the beautiful woodlot that provided most of the timbers for this project) oversee Carding Brook Farm, which has been in their family for generations; to Paul and Amanda at King Hill Farm, where a wide variety of organic produce is grown along with beef, chicken, pork, and eggs; to the Birdsall family of Horsepower Farm, where the bountiful fields and forests are worked with four Suffolk Punch horses; to Mike's friend Peter, who caught the lobsters for our Pumpkin Island feast in the cold waters just offshore. In addition, Julia and I planned our year's garden and poultry production specifically with this project in mind.

We are blessed by the relationships we have with these passionate farmers and growers, and by sharing a mutual appreciation for the gifts of sun, rain, seed, and good loam. We all recognize that when we dig our fingers into the soil, we confess our dependence on the earth. Compassionate farming does not seek to wrest caloric content out of the ground for bare survival. It observes nature and mimics its wisdom. Despite all the technological advances of the 21st century, we cannot turn up our noses at soil in an attempt to synthesize earth's abundance. True *humility* is grounded in the knowledge that it was from humus we were formed, and to humus we will return. Every day as we bow our heads at the dinner table, we are again reminded that it is the soil that produces our daily bread.

MENU

1) Thursday, 8/22

Dinner
Lentil vegetable soup, bread, cheddar block, fruit bowl

2) Friday, 8/23

Breakfast
Oatmeal, toast, jam, cream cheese, hard-boiled eggs, yogurt and berries

Lunch
Greek salad, bread

Snack
Coffee bars

Dinner
Sausage, peppers and onions, rolls, baked beans

3) Saturday, 8/24

Breakfast
Sticky buns, bacon, toast, jam, cream cheese, hard-boiled eggs, yogurt and berries

Lunch
Potato kale soup, bread

Snack
Cheeses, nuts, chocolate

Dinner
Chili, chips, toppings, salad, bread

4) Sunday, 8/25

Breakfast
Coffee cake, toast, jam, cream cheese, hard-boiled eggs, yogurt and berries

Lunch
Spanish tortillas, salad, bread

Snack
Cookies

Dinner
Pork tacos with slaw, cheesy black beans, jalapeño peppers, bread

5) Monday, 8/26

Breakfast
Sausage, bagels, toast, jam, cream cheese, hard-boiled eggs, yogurt and berries

Lunch
Caprese salad with corn, bread

Snack
Popcorn, chocolate

Dinner
Asian salad with noodles, sliced meat, bread

6) Tuesday, 8/27

Breakfast
Oatmeal, chocolate hazelnut spread, toast, jam, cream cheese, hard-boiled eggs, yogurt and berries

Lunch
Fish chowder with bacon garnish, salad, cheese platter, cornbread

Snack
Chocolate beet cake

Dinner
Tinder Hearth pizza, kale salad

7) Wednesday, 8/28

Breakfast
Sausage, farina, hot chocolate, toast, jam, cream cheese, hard-boiled eggs, yogurt and berries

Lunch
Quiche, leftover chowder, bread

Snack
Peach cake

Dinner
Burgers on brioche, potato fries, green beans, homemade pickles

8) Thursday, 8/29

Breakfast
New York bagels and toppings, toast, jam, cream cheese, hard-boiled eggs, yogurt and berries

Lunch
Beet soup, smoked chicken, bread

Snack
Chocolate beet cake

Dinner
Chicken curry, coconut rice, salad, bread

9) Friday, 8/30

Breakfast
Bacon, oat coffee cake, toast, jam, cream cheese, hard-boiled eggs, yogurt and berries

Lunch
Carrot-ginger soup with croutons, salad, bread

Snack
Peach cake

Dinner
Feast at Pumpkin Island: lobster, mussels, corn, green beans

10) Saturday, 8/31

Breakfast
Oatmeal, hot chocolate, toast, jam, cream cheese, hard-boiled eggs, yogurt and berries

Lunch
Black bean salad, corn chips, lobster salad, bread

Snack
Popcorn, honeydew melon with lime

Dinner
Pulled pork sandwiches with slaw, bean hole beans, apple pie and ice cream

11) Sunday, 9/1

Breakfast
Granola and yogurt

Lunch
Leftovers

Dinner
Dinner at a restaurant!

"Recall that whatever lofty things you
might accomplish today, you will do
them only because you first ate
something that grew out of dirt."

– Barbara Kingsolver, "A Good Farmer"

It was clear from the beginning that this was no conventional jobsite – no roar of a generator or shriek of a Skilsaw drowning out conversation. There was nothing here to be heard but the steady thumping of axes, the whisper of saws, and joyful laughter (with the occasional – and somehow fitting – exception of a jobsite speaker playing the Fugees, courtesy of Loïc). And that was the whole point of this thing – the beauty of humans sharing work in honor of nature. It was a rare moment in which there wasn't someone sharing knowledge or a story with others. It would be easy to mistake this project for some kind of reenactment of olde-timey ways, but it was nothing of the sort. This week was a demonstration of convivial and sustainable manual work that is just as relevant in the 21st century as it was in the 12th.

It would have been something else entirely had we relied on the expediency of machines. This was made especially clear on the days throughout the week when the public came to watch. Folks of all ages were lined up at the edge of the worksite, standing in awe to see people using their hands to turn nature into culture. Grandparents, parents, and children alike were visibly moved by the scene. And in our conversations, I got the sense from some that although they thought they had come to watch burly carpenters manhandle massive logs, they discovered instead a display of respectful collaboration – of nature "manifest[ing] itself through the medium of human beings."

"Because folk-craft products are deeply rooted in nature, are created with its support, and are in tune with its ever-changing conditions, we find new and different types of articles being created one after the other, each with its own charm. In this process nature manifests itself through the medium of human beings, resulting in many stylistic variations, each with its own distinctive features."

– Kageo Muraoka and Kichiemon Okamura, *Folk Arts and Crafts of Japan*

CHAPTER 3

An Extension of Our Arms

"It is a quality that has no name. We might call it 'gravity,' but the word does not fully satisfy. Because this quality might accompany the purest, smiling joy. It is the essential quality of the carpenter who stands equal-to-equal before a piece of wood, touches it, caresses it, takes its measure and – far from treating it lightly, harnesses all of its virtues to fulfill his singular purpose."

Antoine de Saint-Exupéry — *Terre des Hommes*

The carpenters brought a variety of shapes of European axes with them, most of which I had never before seen in person.

THURSDAY, AUGUST 22ND

With a rapid pounding in my chest, I pulled into the bus station parking lot to see 15 jet-lagged European travelers eager to find a pillow. Mike and I exchanged greetings and hugs with them before piling into our vans for the hour-long drive back home. Most of our guests slept the whole way.

We stopped first at the *M&T* woodshop for a late-night dinner. Julia had soup and bread at the ready, and everyone savored a bowl or two. It was a quiet meal except for a bit of slurping and hushed French. It wasn't until after dinner, when François Calame, a man whose work I'd come to respect deeply, expressed his appreciation of Julia's food and of our shop space, that it began to dawn on me that the culmination of months of preparation had finally arrived.

While driving our guests over to the two large rental houses where they would be staying for the week, I thought about how much my family had anticipated this event. It had been the topic of dinner conversation for months. Julia and I had begun to learn a bit about French culture, and our boys were enthusiastic to learn new foreign words. This was bound to be a formative event that my little ones would never forget. I laid my head on the pillow that night for the last full night's sleep I'd get in a while.

The next morning was abuzz with energy. As we gathered at the shop for breakfast that first morning, Will Gusakov welcomed the team in English and French and made sure to emphasize that there was no pressure to work that first day. He wanted them to relax and to get over their jet lag. It seemed that the main message he wanted to deliver was, "Take it easy today." The group was broken into seven teams made up of five carpenters apiece, with each team responsible for hewing and joining a particular section of the frame. This would enable everyone to experience each step of the process. The list was studied and the teams met up.

As I was soon to discover, these are some of the most passionate woodworkers around – they'd have to be to spend their vacations hand-hewing timber frames, just for fun. Soon after everyone met with their teams, they set to work sharpening tools and making their way down to the hewing stations to begin converting logs to timbers.

Up to this point, I confess I felt uneasy each time I looked at those piles of logs. I couldn't help wondering, "Is this really possible?" The sheer mass of material to be removed was intimidating – these logs were huge, and there were tons of them.

But, to my surprise, before I could even make heads or tails of the work-flow or hardly anyone's name, I saw a thick bed of wood chips mounting underfoot, and round, ragged logs turning into smooth, square timbers.

HEWING

The teams set the logs on "bunks" to keep their axes out of the dirt while hewing. Putting the work up on these red pine offcuts gave the carpenters at least a foot of clearance to the ground and raised the work higher. Some of the bunks had notches hewn into them to help cradle the logs, but most did not. Each log was secured from rolling with log dogs (essentially, big iron staples) on the opposite side of the face to be hewn. These log dogs were each unique in size and shape, being mostly blacksmith-made.

To lay out lines for hewing, the timber's cross-sectional dimensions were drawn onto both ends of the log, with their sides established plumb. The Americans typically used their spirit levels to do this, but some of the French carpenters used their plumb bobs to establish these lines. Once the ends were drawn, they were connected down the length of the log with the snap of a chalk line, making a straight timber from the natural, irregular tree. In most cases, the carpenters

peeled a strip of bark only where the lines would be snapped, rather than peeling the entire log. This served two purposes: First, it saved labor because peeling bark in areas that were going to be hewn away would be wasted energy, and second, the bark provided grip for standing on when working the log underfoot. Freshly peeled logs are slippery.

The lines were snapped carefully. Although the subtleties of using a chalk line are something I never really thought too much about, when snapping lines on irregular pieces (such as logs), it is critically important to lift the string exactly plumb so that it is in plane with the sides of the timber, otherwise the line will snap out of plane in low spots. To ensure that the taut line was plumb before letting it go, another carpenter would sight the line for them. "No, a little to the left. A little back. There." Snap! This way, a dead straight line could be achieved no matter the topography down the length of the tree. In addition to a trained eye, squares and levels were sometimes used to ensure that the line was plumb before snapping.

TOP: Loïc Desmonts peels bark for snapping chalk lines.

RIGHT: Paul Cookson and Louis Jamin kerf the log with a two-man crosscut saw.

BOTTOM: François Calame chops notches down the length of the log to remove the bulk of the waste.

With the finished member marked out, all that was left was to remove everything that wasn't the timber.

This was accomplished in three steps: scoring/notching, joggling, and hewing. The first step is all about providing cross-grain stop cuts via regular kerfing with the two-man cross-cut saw or by notching with the axe down the length of the log. The waste areas between the notches are then "joggled" off the log by swinging a long-handled felling axe parallel to the tree's fibers. Ideally, this coarse stage leaves no more than 1/2" of material to remove with the hewing axe (which is the axe equivalent to the smoothing plane).

This joggling process is a bit awkward to get used to at first, because it is often done while standing on top of the log, swinging a long-handled felling axe beneath your feet. Maintaining your balance while guiding a 4"-wide bit on a 36"-long handle at the end of your fully extended arms requires a considerable amount of skill. Of course, these folks made it look easy, and it was only when I jumped on for a turn that I realized what it actually takes to nail this. There is no instruction book or how-to guide that can give secret tips that will enable you to bypass years of practice. This kind of work is all about your brain and hands getting to know that tool.

In *The Glass Cage: Automation and Us*, author Nicholas Carr discusses a fascinating area of neuroscience research called "embodied cognition." He explains that scientists have found that the "workings [of the brain and body] are interwoven to a degree far beyond what we assume. The biological processes that constitute 'thinking' emerge not just from neural computations in the skull but from actions and sensory perceptions of the entire body." He gives the retina as one example and says it "isn't a passive sensor sending raw data to the brain, as was once assumed; it actively shapes what we see. The eye has smarts of its own."

The idea that our understanding of our surroundings is formed not only in our brains, but throughout our whole bodies, is consequential to our relationship with our tools. Carr explains that "our bodies and brains are quick to bring tools and other artifacts into our thought processes – to treat things, neurologically, as parts of our selves. If you walk with a cane or work with a hammer or fight with a sword, your brain will incorporate the tools into its neuronal map of your body." [2]

What Carr is telling us is that through disciplined practice, our brains begin to think of hand-held tools – such as saws, planes, or axes – as if they really *are* an extension of our arms. This also might shed scientific light on a phenomenon that many woodworkers may have thought too subjective and emotional to repeat within earshot of the more cynical among us: the idea that using hand tools make us feel a closer "connection" to the material we work. Based on the findings of these scientists, that might actually be true.

This research makes me wonder if neuron mapping might also be a part of the reason that we become so partial to our own tools. We attune ourselves to the subtleties of the handles' length, shape, thickness, and even facets, and these cues provide information that aids our brains in the mapping process. It's like the notorious partiality that professional baseball players develop for their bats. "If a bat doesn't feel right to… outfielder Bryce Harper, he'll toss it right away. Harper can just tell it's all wrong." [3]

When it comes to my personal tools, I've long believed that their unrefined and faceted handles help me to better engage my work. Every little idiosyncrasy gives my brain a positive reference for orientation and cutting angle. When using tools with round, smooth handles, I am completely dependent on visual confirmation to use them accurately. This limitation introduces an element of doubt into the workflow, and can slow things down – exactly the kind of experience a working craftsman wants to avoid.

At the CSF project in Maine, the carpenters' hewing abilities were even more impressive than their joggling – they split the line with their axes all day long as if it was nothing. It was clear that they have spent many hours with these tools, and each axe's handmade uniqueness strengthened the connection between artisan and tool. The axes on-site were highly individual and varied tremendously from tradition to tradition, but most were French, American, Swedish, or German. Many of the examples we had on-site had a bevel on only one side. The idea with this style is that the "flat" back (actually slightly convex in both directions) guides the tool in creating a flat surface on the timber.

"Axe Handles"
By Gary Snyder

One afternoon the last week in April
Showing Kai how to throw a hatchet
One-half turn and it sticks in a stump.
He recalls the hatchet-head
Without a handle, in the shop
And go gets it, and wants it for his own.
A broken-off axe handle behind the door
Is long enough for a hatchet,
We cut it to length and take it
With the hatchet head
And working hatchet, to the wood block.
There I begin to shape the old handle
With the hatchet, and the phrase
First learned from Ezra Pound
Rings in my ears!
"When making an axe handle
      the pattern is not far off."
And I say this to Kai
"Look: We'll shape the handle
By checking the handle
Of the axe we cut with—"
And he sees. And I hear it again:
It's in Lu Ji's *Wên Fu*, fourth century
A.D. "Essay on Literature"— in the
Preface: "In making the handle
Of an axe
By cutting wood with an axe
The model is indeed near at hand."
My teacher Shih-hsiang Chen
Translated that and taught it years ago
And I see: Pound was an axe,
Chen was an axe, I am an axe
And my son a handle, soon
To be shaping again, model
And tool, craft of culture,
How we go on.

*This poem was read by Hank Silver at
one of the morning meetings.*

One of the carpenters, Andy Hyde, explained to me that he was taught to hew systematically at a diagonal downwards, attempting to keep a sheet of material hanging on the log rather than making a million little chips. The reason for this is that the hanging material guides the tool along a straight path down the face. The single-bevel axe requires an offset handle in order to prevent bashing your knuckles on the timber as you hew. Although the single bevel was used in many traditions, the German *breitbeil* (what we call a "goosewing" axe in America) is Andy's tool of choice. Andy explained to me that the carefully engineered geometry of the tool so quickly makes the work feel natural. This may be why many new hewers gravitate to the *breitbeil*.

But other carpenters swear by double-bevel hewing axes. On Sunday night, Gustave Rémon gave a presentation of his research into medieval French axes. He talked about the key features he's studied in examples in his collection and those of museums around Europe. The presentation ended with a description of the process of forging and using a replica socketed axe made by Simon Luquet, a blacksmith from Alsace, France. Gustave affectionately calls this axe his "baby." He talked about the versatility of the design, explaining that it can be used for everything from the carving of spoons to the building of cathedrals.

Gustave might be more obsessed with axes than anyone I've ever met. His passion runs so deep that he prefers to use nothing but his axe to build timber frames. He describes the saw as a specialist tool that "enslaves" the user. But the axe, in contrast, can be used to accomplish many different tasks, and Gustave sees this flexibility as allowing a great degree of artisanal freedom. During the Maine project, Gustave shaped several tenons with nothing more than his "baby" – guided by hand and eye. He even formed the tenons' shoulders with careful axe chops. The skill of cutting cross-grain shoulders with an axe is another level of craftsmanship.

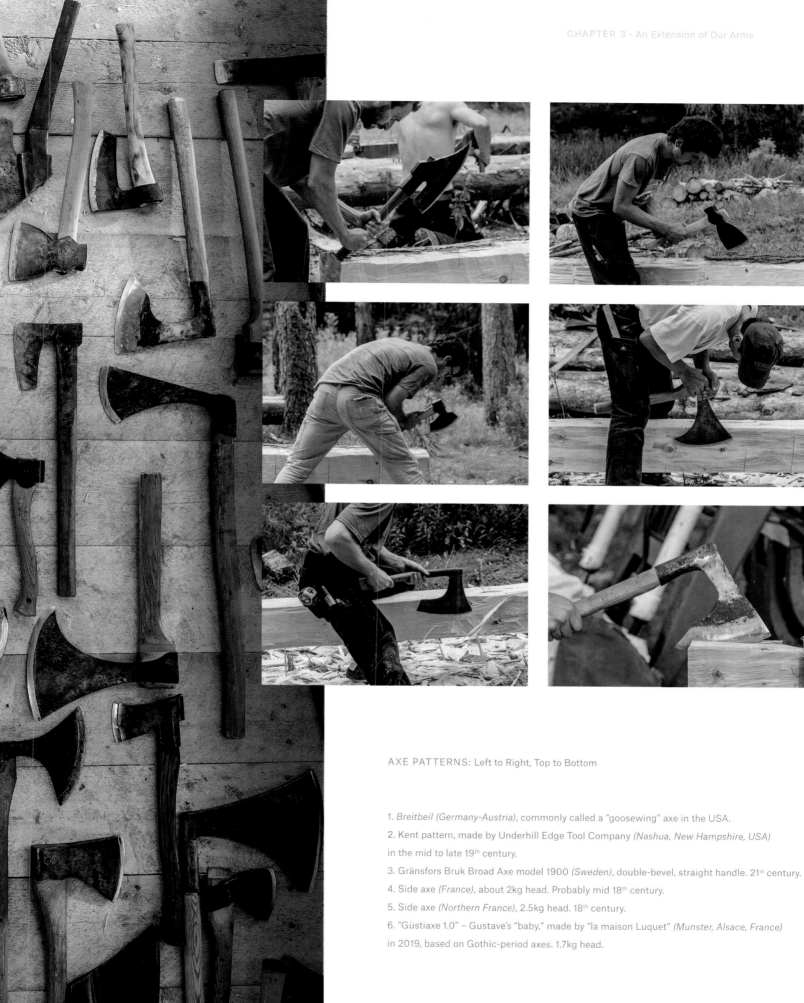

AXE PATTERNS: Left to Right, Top to Bottom

1. *Breitbeil (Germany-Austria)*, commonly called a "goosewing" axe in the USA.

2. Kent pattern, made by Underhill Edge Tool Company *(Nashua, New Hampshire, USA)* in the mid to late 19th century.

3. Gränsfors Bruk Broad Axe model 1900 *(Sweden)*, double-bevel, straight handle. 21st century.

4. Side axe *(France)*, about 2kg head. Probably mid 18th century.

5. Side axe *(Northern France)*, 2.5kg head. 18th century.

6. "Güstiaxe 1.0" – Gustave's "baby," made by "la maison Luquet" *(Munster, Alsace, France)* in 2019, based on Gothic-period axes. 1.7kg head.

I wish I could tell you exactly how long it took to hew one 8" x 8" timber, but in all honesty I was so astonished at how fast everything happened that the clock was an afterthought. Mike said he clocked Gustave hewing the single flat on a 14' rafter at about two minutes. Loïc calculated the average speed of hewing on this project to be 1.19m²/person-hour. By this math, this means that from rough log to finished timber, an 8" x 8" x 12' post took somewhere around three hours to produce.

I have never seen anything more awe-inspiring than this team of people hewing the entire frame in little over two days of labor. And, by all accounts, this was at a pretty casual pace. After the eight days of construction, several of the carpenters came up with independent estimates of the time they would need to build this frame with the same methods. The average bid was four person-months (640 hours) – two people for two months. This is the kind of efficiency that skill can achieve.

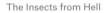

The Insects from Hell

The quantity of mosquitos on the worksite was unbelievable, but even more entertaining were the bugs they call "no-see-ums." They would arrive every evening at precisely 5:00 p.m., and at that time, I saw all of the carpenters suddenly coming up out of the forest, slapping themselves. This signaled the end of the work-day. For the stragglers, like Andy Hyde, it was hilarious to see them gesticulate in all directions, being driven crazy by these "insects from hell."

To combat the mosquitoes, Will Lisak made a batch of birch tar before coming up. As I understand, the odor repels them. It was incredibly effective. Will joked, "You'll see – the smell even drives people away!" This was true, too, with the exception of Kinga Kłusak who approached us saying: "Mmmm, you guys smell like good Polish sausages!"

– Loïc Desmonts, *France*

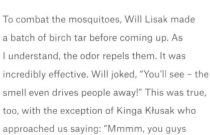

CHAPTER 4

Joyful Engagement

"[I]n spite of all this toil – perhaps, in a sense, because of it – work is a good thing for man. . . . It is not only good in the sense that it is useful or something to enjoy; it is also good as being something worthy, that is to say, something that corresponds to man's dignity, that expresses this dignity and increases it. If one wishes to define more clearly the ethical meaning of work, it is this truth that one must particularly keep in mind. Work is a good thing for man – a good thing for his humanity – because through work man not only transforms nature, adapting it to his own needs, but he also achieves fulfilment as a human being and indeed, in a sense, becomes 'more a human being.'"

John Paul II – *Laborem Exercens*

BELOW: Square-rule Layout

The hallmark of square-rule layout is the series
of reductions in the timber at joinery locations.
These reductions bring the mating surfaces
of the timber to a regular depth, which is
referenced off of a straight edge or snapped
chalk line. This system enables the carpenter
to cut identical shoulder-to-shoulder distances
on like components, gaining the advantages
of interchangeability. The scribing method, in
contrast, does not use these reductions, and
therefore every component is custom-fit to
its mating members.

SATURDAY, AUGUST 24TH

On day three of our project, the carpenters were laying out joinery, and by day four, tenons emerged and mortises were chopped. The layout was a focal point of this project because one of the major objectives was to have the foreign crew learn the American square-rule method. This system relies on cutting shoulder reductions to a fixed depth, which accommodates the irregularities of hewn or rough-sawn surfaces. It's often described as envisioning the "ideal timber within." Because a hand-hewn or rough-sawn 8" x 8" post is potentially 1/4" smaller or larger at any point, a reference edge or line is designated, and shoulder reductions are cut to the "ideal timber" diameter of, say, 7". By making these reductions all the same depth from the reference, you know exactly the shoulder-to-shoulder measurement for the post's mating timbers. This system couldn't be more different than the French method of scribing the timbers to their mating members using plumb bobs. (Refer to chapter six for a description of this method.) I was delighted to watch the sharing and exchange of information from so many skilled craftspeople from different traditions.

There were also some interesting tools on site that I never get to see in my furniture work. The most familiar of these to Americans was the boring machine, a wooden or iron hand-cranked portable drill press for removing waste from mortises. The boring machine is essentially a jig for a self-feeding screw auger. Once the bit is positioned, the carpenter sits on the base of the tool and cranks the two handles 'round and 'round, driving the bit into the wood. There are all sorts of bells and whistles that have been offered with these over the years – depth gauges and stops, adjustability for angles other than 90°, and gears for withdrawing the bit after reaching depth. The boring machine is believed to be an American invention based on early 19th-century patent records. It seemed that most of the Europeans had never used this tool before; they usually rely on t-handled augers for this job. One of the carpenters, Victor Calame, said that the boring machine is much less tiring to use than the t-auger. Still, some t-handled augers found use on the jobsite.

Almost completely unfamiliar to Americans is the *besaiguë* (pronounced bees-ay-goo), a French combination slick and mortise chisel. In use, the *besaiguë* rests on the shoulder and one hand grasps the perpendicular handle while the other guides the blade. Gustave, who brought his experimental folding version, said the tool is much easier to use on timbers sitting on low bunks than on the taller, American sawhorses we used on this project. This is because the *besaiguë* depends on the weight of the artisan to cut – it's not mallet-driven. Because these are such large tools, only Gustave's custom folding version came along from overseas, but this tool usually features prominently at CSF job sites.

Evan Sachs uses one of the several
boring machines we had on the jobsite.

ABOVE: Skip Dewhirst bores the waste out of a mortise with a t-handled auger.

RIGHT: Gustave Rémon pares waste from the walls of a mortise with his *besaiguë*.

TOP: The team whipped up a quick trestle with red pine offcuts. With its feet staked into the ground, this design was a sturdy solution for such a short-term project.

BOTTOM: Wedges in the end kerf kept the saw blade from getting pinched as the sawyers progressed down the line.

And then there was the pitsaw. A few months before the project, Will Lisak sourced a batch of new pitsaws from Sheffield, England, made by E. Garlick and Son. Both he and I had been looking to get our own saws for a while, so we pitched in with a few other friends to place an order for a handful (and save on international shipping costs). We hadn't even had time to try it out before CSF arrived, but there were many folks on-site with serious experience with pitsaws, and they knew what kind of adjustments could be made to optimize the saw tooth geometry for our purposes. The saw plate came without handles, so during the project I jumped on the spring-pole lathe to turn out a couple "saw boxes," two-handled wooden blocks wedged onto the plate. The wedged saw box was traditionally used only on the bottom of the saw so that the handle could be removed to pull the plate out of the kerf, if needed. Because I didn't yet have a top tiller handle, a second saw box filled the need in a pinch. The carpenters used this beefy 7'-long saw to rip several of the curved hardwood braces so that they could be installed in a bookmatched orientation in the frame.

Will Lisak, Loïc Desmonts, Mike Updegraff, and Asher Finch rigged up a trestle next to two trees they'd connected with a crossmember, ratchet-strapped tight. The timber to be sawn was hoisted up onto the trestle and crossbeam and secured, so that one carpenter was up on the trestle holding the top handle while the other was underneath, on the ground. I heard mixed comments about pitsawing from the carpenters – some loved the meditative up-and-down motion, but others seemed to prefer hewing all day. All in all, it appeared that swinging axes was more physically exhausting than working the pitsaw – the hewers were the ones covered in sweat.

The Farmer and His Children

Work hard, sweat all you can:
Riches is what counts the least.
A rich farmer, sensing his impending death,
Called for his children, and spoke to them without witnesses.
Do not sell the inheritance left by our parents, he said,
As a treasure is hidden in it.
I do not know where, but with a bit of courage
You will find it, you will figure it out.
Go search the field when summer ends.
Dig, scratch, plow, leave no earth unturned
Anywhere your hands can reach.
After the father's death, the sons worked the field
Everywhere, over and over again, so that within a year
It produced more than ever before.
There was no money to be found, but the father had been wise
To show them before his death
That work is a treasure.

– Jean de La Fontaine,
Fables de La Fontaine (1668)

JOYFUL ENGAGEMENT

If I had to describe the spirit of the crew during the construction in one word, it would be "joy." Everyone took their work seriously, yes, but they also looked like they were having the time of their lives. So many said that even though they may be professional timber framers, they look forward to these yearly CSF vacations, in which they are unfettered by the usual economic constraint of the bottom line, to work and sweat to their hearts' content. Many concurred with Will Gusakov's reflection that this was the type of work they *want* to do.

There is joy to be found in good work that is done well, but if we accept the contemporary paradigm that all physical work is inherently onerous, we tacitly affirm that withdrawal from this activity is desirable. We fill the void with an indiscriminate embrace of the commodities of convenience, forgetting that there is indeed something about manual labor, especially when done alongside others, that seems to fulfill our humanity. But it is easy to lose sight of this while living in a culture of comfort and detachment from the beautiful realities of raw, gritty life – such necessities as the tending of farm animals and construction of buildings.

But doesn't technology make our lives better?

Yes and no. Ever since the Industrial Revolution, the fundamental aim of technological progress has been the procurement of relief from life's burdens through devices, which can be defined as the means by which commodities are conveyed (speakers bring us music, microwaves provide warm meals, telephones facilitate communication). At the extreme end of this technological trajectory, food is procured from a can by an electric can opener, and we perform our daily work sitting in a cushy chair, staring into a computer screen. We are told it is dangerous to bend or lift or exert ourselves. And because we are afraid to sweat, we smother ourselves with antiperspirants. Our bodies become inconsequential.

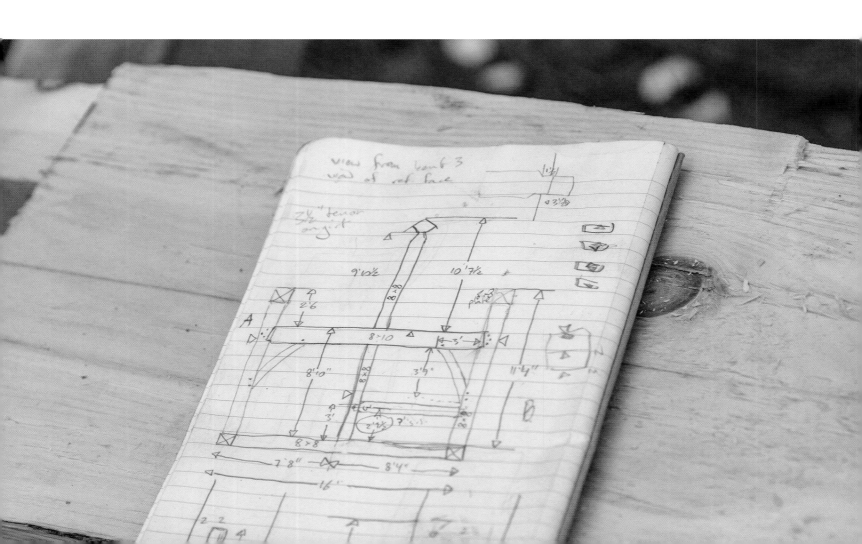

When it comes to our physical burdens, industrial and post-industrial technologies provide relief through various forms of mechanization, automation, and digitization. In the 21st century, this manifests in the continual redesigning of our devices, in order that they be increasingly more "intuitive" through simplifying the user interface. Our ease of mind as consumers is achieved when the designers reduce our responsibilities and options. We can see this clearly in our highly sophisticated digital devices encased in the smooth lines of hard plastic, leaving us only a few buttons to engage with.

The development of the simple interface is undoubtedly a blessing in that it enables us to utilize powerful tools without specialized knowledge. It makes our work fast, accurate, and efficient. But one of the tradeoffs to outsourcing our competence to specialists is that our need to mentally engage diminishes. We become no longer cognizant of the intricacies of the stuff we use on a daily basis. In the loss of our sensibility, we lose interest. We become disengaged. [4]

Take, for example, the humble road trip. There are two different ways to plan for a long drive, and the first way is to depend on the paper map. The paper map lays out the whole region with all the highways and backroads and shows how they relate to one another. This analog technology empowers the driver to understand the intersections, so that when each is crossed, the whole picture remains in view. The map undoubtedly involves time investment to study the roads and make decisions about the best route, but once the driver has engaged with the map and driven the roads studied, it is virtually impossible to get lost again. The most vivid memory I have of this is from my honeymoon, in which my wife and I drove from Maine through Canada to Minnesota, where we moved into our first apartment. We spent two weeks forging our way through foreign territory with nothing but the map to guide us. We both have distinct memories of that trip and all the precarious and hilarious backways we found. Our sense of that place remains strong.

Compare this to the GPS-guided trip so many of us have become accustomed to. We copy and paste the address of our destination (or allow the app to auto-fill it from the search bar), fire the ignition, and turn off our brains. We no longer have to look at the big map to chart our course across the country because we have faith that the device will not lead us astray. Our only job at the wheel is to turn left when Google tells us to turn left. As long as we obey, we will arrive safely (and in the best time). Though this method undeniably makes our travel efficient, it does so at the cost of engagement. Our minds disengage from the roads, the names of towns, and (when we're engrossed in the latest podcasts) the beautiful scenery around us. The next thing we know, "Your destination is on the left," and we have no memory of which roads we just drove on all day. The first time I became aware of this phenomenon, it was just after having arrived at my destination and my host asked, "So, which way did you take? Was it down through so-and-so or did you take the upper route around it?" I was dreadfully embarrassed that I did not know. Talk about disengagement!

And this kind of detachment from a sense of place is emotionally dislocating. When we cut ourselves off from the reality around us, we can feel useless and disabled to take care of ourselves. We wish we understood the roads better. We covet the skills to build and fix our own possessions. And this helplessness is socially dislocating too, because we no longer know where we fit in society. Our sense of self-worth diminishes when our devices do better for us what we used to do for ourselves. And now, especially with the emergence of the self-driving car, we're losing our place and losing our joy.

Mihaly Csikszentmihalyi's now-famous analysis of what he calls "flow" explains that there is a direct relationship between our skill, the challenge we set before ourselves, and our happiness. A proper balance between skill and challenge must be maintained, because if the challenge at hand exceeds our skill set by too much, discouragement sets in, or if our abilities far exceed what the task demands of us, we are afflicted with boredom. Both lead us to discontent. Csikszentmihalyi tells us that joy can be found in the constant pursuit of higher skills that demand ever-higher challenges. Through this process of skillful engagement, we grow in competence and personal satisfaction. [5]

But do not think that happiness is relevant only to our leisure activities. Wendell Berry has lamented that "more and more, we take for granted that work must be destitute of pleasure" and that we experience pleasure only off the clock, in the realm of hobbies. He warns that the disengaging influences of mechanization and automation "divide us ever more from our work and our products – and, in the process, from one another and the world." [6] We were not designed to be sedentary creatures – we have been gifted with bodies that require motion, muscles that demand to be flexed, and minds that crave challenge. Cutting ourselves off from manual activity smothers us by dulling our appreciation for the world and our call to work in it.

"For all the hundreds of thousands of years that man has lived on this earth he has engaged in manual work. As a result, there has developed an intimate, close and unbreakable interaction between manual work and man's moral character. The past two and a half centuries of machinery have not broken this connection. Man needs hand work to maintain his happiness and sanity.

"Work with the hands gives immediate and tangible results. It causes a prompt, perceptible change in one's thinking and feeling. It therefore gives an immediate sense of accomplishment and satisfaction, and the encouragement to do it again and continue to do so as to win still further concrete results. It is self-validating." [7]

"The civilized man has built a coach, but has lost the use of his feet. He is supported on crutches, but lacks so much support of muscle. He has a fine Geneva watch, but he fails of the skill to tell the hour by the sun. . . . and it may be a question whether machinery does not encumber..."

– Ralph Waldo Emerson, *Self-Reliance*

Learning to engage with the world through handcraft is one of the most powerful ways to cultivate joy in this life. Seeing the satisfaction blazoned across the faces of these carpenters couldn't have made this point any more clear to me. These are engaged people, and in their work, they brim with joy. Projects like this are a vivid reminder that "work is a good thing for man," and that it is possible to envision a future that embraces the benefits of modern technology without its dehumanizing tendencies. Let us never forget in our pursuit of technological development, that the well-being of our humanity will be ignored only to our detriment.

And when we as individuals come to terms with concrete reality on a daily basis, we will begin to find that the solutions to some of our social, spiritual, economic, and ecological problems may not be as complicated as we think. Take a step back from the frenzy. Involve yourself in the raw stuff of life. If we take the time to do this, we will find that the satisfaction that comes through deep engagement with the world around us outshines the fleeting pleasures of consumerism. It is a way of being in the world that points to a humane future in which a work of joy is possible.

CHAPTER 5
With Such Facility

"It has still to be proved that displacement of the hand by the machine is a blessing in every case. . . . The machinery method is no doubt easy. But it is not necessarily a blessing on that account. The descent to a certain place is easy but dangerous. The method of the hand is a blessing, in the present case at any rate, because it is hard. If the craze for the machinery method continues, it is highly likely that a time will come when we shall be so incapacitated and weak that we shall begin to curse ourselves for having forgotten the use of the living machines given to us by God. . . . We should not use machinery for producing things which we can produce without its aid and have got the capacity to do so. . . . If I can produce my things myself, I become my master and so need no machinery."

Mahatma Gandhi — *Hind Swaraj and Other Writings* [8]

TUESDAY, AUGUST 27TH

By Tuesday morning, the emphasis was on finishing the square-rule mortises and tenons. The carpenters focused particularly on the tamarack sill system, because once that was installed, the deck could be used for assembling the bents to scribe the braces. We chose tamarack ("hackmatack," or even "hack," it's called in New England) for the sills because it is especially rot-resistant. Although not an uncommon tree around Maine, these large, straight trees are harder to come by, and nothing in Jon's woodlot was even close to what we needed. Fortunately, Josh Wehrwein, a mutual friend of ours, had the perfect stand of hack on his property just up the road. When Jon explored this stand, he remarked that he'd not seen bigger, straighter tamarack anywhere else in the area. These were special trees that deserved to be put to noble use. Josh agreed to sell the trees, which, due to inordinate amounts of mud, were only accessible by tractor.

As Jon limbed the fallen trees, he was disappointed to find that the absolute maximum length he could get out of one of the two logs was 6" shorter than we needed for the 26' sill pieces called for. Although we could have scarfed the sill with another piece to obtain our goal of 26', we ultimately decided it would be better to shorten the building by 1' to give us one-piece sills. This meant that, besides needing to adjust some of the shoulder-to-shoulder measurements of the timbers, we had to move two of the granite blocks 1' at one gable end. This was a simple fix and a sensible tradeoff – sacrificing only a little square footage to get the best structural configuration.

Everyone seemed to agree that hewing the hackmatack was much different than hewing the white pine. It was noticeably harder – harder to work and harder on tool edges. The French carpenters didn't feel the strain as much as the Americans, though, because they are used to hewing oak, a wood much tougher than our softwoods.

"If we meet with knotty pieces of timber, and we think to master them by force and violence, and hew them to pieces, they may not only prove too hard for us, but the attempt may turn to our own damage. . . . Let wisdom direct to gentle methods and forbear violent ones. Wisdom will teach us to whet the tool we are to make use of, rather than, by leaving it blunt, oblige ourselves to exert so much the more strength. We might save ourselves a great deal of labour, and prevent a great deal of danger, if we did whet before we cut..."

– Matthew Henry, *Complete Commentary*

The sill beams were carried to the foundation blocks, and everything was carefully leveled before the pegs were driven. The joists were hewn only on one face, leaving the round log underneath. This standard historic practice is pure practicality. There's no reason to hew a surface that will never receive joinery, and many historic New England cellars and attics show this expediency. Once the joists were dropped into their half-lap mortises, the 2"-thick spruce decking was nailed down.

After the last board was attached, Gustave and Miles were given the honor of hewing it flush to the sill. Everyone gathered around to watch these two go at it full-bore. The dinner bell rang as the deck was completed, and we feasted with gratitude for another successful day's work.

Rather than ripping the length of
the last floorboard with a saw, a pair
of axes made quick work of it – and
looked like a bunch of fun.

"By becoming involved in the shaping of things around us, we grow in self-confidence and knowledge with a resulting growth in security. By needing less ourselves, we make more of the world's store available to those in want. Covetousness is reduced when we have simple things that others can easily obtain for themselves. The simpler something is to make, the more easily it can be replaced and the less we are dependent on special skills, materials, or markets. So simplicity is not just a matter of doing more with less, or spending less, or using less of the world's resources; it is a matter of freedom."

– William Coperthwaite, *A Handmade Life*

A MATTER OF FREEDOM

It was a surreal sight, the deck of the first floor laid in place where it is destined to remain for the next several hundred years. At dinner that night, I looked at these carpenters a little differently. I had a heightened sense of appreciation for these men and women who were carefully and skilfully crafting a building to last well beyond our lifetimes. The axe, the saw, and the chisel free these folks from dependence on corded machinery or complex and specialized tools. Many of their tools are either antiques with the patina from generations of care, or were made by individual blacksmiths or small firms. With their simple tools, these carpenters have the ability to shape the world around them – from such basic tasks as making leather sheaths for their axes, to carving their own eating utensils, to grand projects on the scale of building their own houses.

It was inspiring to see a group of people have such facility with their tools, able to make just about anything they needed on site. If a handle broke, it only took a few minutes to make a new one. If the teeth of a crosscut saw needed to be modified, files were brought out to a saw vise in the yard. A dull saw or a broken tooth doesn't send this crew running to the big-box store to purchase another disposable replacement. It seemed to me that the breadth of experience and depth of knowledge empower them to tackle just about anything.

The consumerist impulse was conspicuously absent from this job. Although many present seemed happy to participate in the global economy, what distinguishes them in my mind is that they seem genuinely able to choose between purchasing something or making it themselves. This is a breath of fresh air, because too many of us feel disempowered by our dependence on commercially supplied devices, whether it be a new app, dovetail jig, or honing contraption. Some of us wish we could shed these

unnecessary accoutrements, and when we're fed sales pitches that promise professional results in three easy payments, we feel manipulated and demeaned. The danger with mass production is that, although it is able to reliably produce quality goods, dependence on it undermines the opportunity for individuals to learn to make do or make their own. It can inhibit the development of the individual.

Something that got passed around the jobsite on more than one occasion was the word "sabotage." Several of the carpenters said they thought of working local materials with hand tools as a sort of sabotage to consumerist culture. I thought this analogy was particularly fitting because of the word's French origin, roughly translating to "wooden-shoeing." Historian John Spargo has traced the first use of the word to late-19th-century authors Émile Pouget and Paul Delassale in their attempt to translate into French the Scottish phrase *Ca' Canny*, a name used for the policy of disgruntled British workers who deliberately slowed their work. [9] Spargo compared the term with the English slang

"The Leader of the Luddites" Published in May 1812 by Messrs. Walker and Knight, Sweetings Alley, Royal Exchange. Public Domain. Wikimedia Commons.

"soldiering" – a reference to workers slacking at the job as a means of reducing profitability for the factory owners.

He explained that the word "sabotage" was likely chosen by Pouget and Delassale because "[i]n France, especially in the rural districts, it has long been the custom to liken the slow and clumsy worker to one wearing wooden shoes, called 'sabots.' The phrase, *Travailler a coups de sabots*, to work as one wearing wooden shoes, has long been used with reference to the slow and clumsy worker, the 'old soldier' as they say in England. . . . The idea is obvious: the peasant with heavy wooden shoes walks clumsily and slowly in comparison with those who wear shoes of leather." [10]

The core idea of sabotage is to hit the employer in the pocketbook. Throughout history there have been all sorts of sabotage to industry – some violent and destructive (as done by the Luddites of early 19th-century Britain), and others simply involving worker noncompliance or obstruction of productivity. Spargo mentions that over time, a movement developed which was described as "constructive sabotage," a variety that focused on striking over the dishonest actions of companies – adulterating products, for example. Because Spargo himself was opposed to the practice of destructive sabotage as a method of achieving positive change, he endorsed this nonviolent spirit.

This idea of opting out of the industrial system as a form of resistance has several points of connection to *Swadeshi*, the movement led by Mahatma Gandhi in the first half of the 20th century. As part of the larger (ultimately successful) movement for Indian independence, this "constructive program," as he called it, encouraged Indian citizens to confine their economic support to local artisans and industries in order to sever their dependence on British industry. Gandhi's *swadeshi* was not conceived of as vengeful boycott, but rather as a "religious principle" that he hoped would make every village "a self-supporting and self-contained unit, exchanging only such necessary commodities with other villages as are not locally producible." [11] *Swadeshi* became a practical ideal when Gandhi began to promote local production of *khadi*, a handspun, handwoven cloth. He was known for spending much time at his spinning wheel, and it ultimately became the symbol for the decentralizing efforts of the movement. "The *charkha*, or spinning wheel, was the physical embodiment and symbol of Gandhi's constructive program. It represents Swadeshi, self-sufficiency, and at the same time interdependence, because the wheel is at the center of a network of cotton growers, carders, weavers, distributors, and users. It also embodied the dignity of labor, equality, unity . . ." [12]

Mahatma Gandhi's focus on local *khadi* production as an essential component of the push for Indian independence was not without controversy, being spurned as technologically regressive. But Gandhi knew that protests were not enough, and if there was to be any way forward in the struggle for independence, a positive alternative would have to be set forth.

Those of us who want to take a step back to build a life of broadening and rising competence can take these examples to heart. Carpenters Without Borders demonstrates part of what it looks like to move toward independence from industrial supply. Making use of such basic things as local materials, communal work, and manual tools minimizes our reliance on outside specialists and imported goods. It is an approach that is proportionate to small-scale and individual needs.

Some people work hard to make an impact in the world through political action – picketing, protesting, and campaigning. But author Wendell Berry has maintained that "for others, there is the possibility of a protest that is more complex and permanent, public in effect but private in its motive and implementation: they can *live* in protest. I have in mind a sort of personal secession from the encroaching institutional machinery of destruction and waste and violence.... Another possibility, equally necessary, and in the long run richer in promise, is to remove oneself as far as possible from complicity in the evils one is protesting, and to discover alternative possibilities. To make public protests against an evil, and yet live in dependence on and in support of the way of life that is the source of the evil, is an obvious contradiction and a dangerous one.... If one feels endangered by meaninglessness, then one is under an obligation to refuse meaningless pleasure and to resist meaningless work, and to give up the moral comfort and the excuses of the mentality of specialization." [13]

"Man is most free when his tools are proportionate to his needs."

– Sōetsu Yanagi, *The Unknown Craftsman*

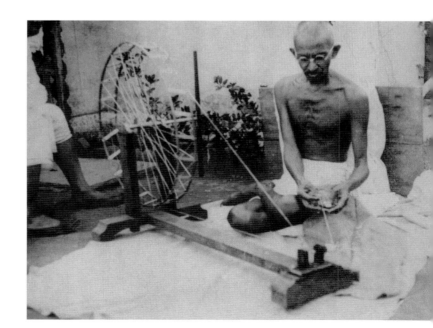

Mahatma Gandhi spinning at his wheel.
Wikimedia Commons.

"The important thing we need is not the machine,
it's what I have in my hands:
my skills. "

For many of the folks working on this timber frame project, the axe was and is the "physical embodiment and symbol" of these "alternative possibilities" that are available to us. The simple act of taking up tools is a trailhead to the path toward independence. With them, we wield the means to build the world we want to see. It is a small thing to learn to use an axe. But a life comprised of many such down-to-earth and constructive decisions is the framework for a new way of seeing the world – one rooted in empowerment, compassion, and freedom.

As one of the CSF carpenters, Florian Carpentier, put it,

"[The axe is] one of the most basic tools since humanity [came into being]. And with just these few tools, some of them I am able to make myself, I can build comfortable, durable houses to shelter people. Many people are nowadays in a quest for meaning in their life. They don't see the point anymore in working so much, to earn so much money, to spend so much money, to have so little time for family and friends and themselves. You have the slow food movement; we are the slow construction movement. It's a provocation. It's like sabotage to the big machine. We show that we are able to go against the machine at our little level. But we have an impact. Even though it's small, we have an impact, and we must use it. It's not like I will save the world with my timber frames, but at least I do not destroy the world, which is already very good.

"Whatever you can do to make sabotage, you have to do it. [For my part,] I participate in creating good living conditions for people who will live in my houses, and I contribute to maintain the balance of nature and the ecosystem by using local trees, low technologies, and low-impact processes. This is meaningful because the important thing we need is not the machine, it's what I have in my hands: my skills. The human is put back in the central position in the process of building."

CHAPTER 6

Beyond Borders

"If it is true that folk wisdom is our basic wealth, the chief insurance of a culture's worth, then we are nearly bankrupt. Traditional knowledge is disappearing at an accelerating rate, as the creations of local craftspeople are replaced by factory-made products, which are not designed with a concern for the improvement of human life but merely for profit. We need to be collecting as many examples as possible of the old knowledge and skill, before they are forgotten and lost forever."

William Coperthwaite — *A Handmade Life*

WEDNESDAY, AUGUST 28TH

Having the deck in place on Wednesday morning enabled the carpenters to progress to the next step: scribing the curved braces into the bents. In turn, each team assembled their assigned bent horizontally on the deck, and the whole thing was then leveled to establish a flat reference plane. This level plane enabled to carpenters to lay the curved braces on top of the bent in their positions and transfer the shoulders, relying on a plumb line instead of a square. Transferring layout like this is an ancient but effective method for dealing with the irregularities of hewn timber. Square-rule and scribing are two different ways to accomplish this, but squares are more dependent on regular material. Plumb bobs will always reference the center of the earth, no matter where they're hanging.

Hanging a plumb line from the upper face of a brace to the lower face of a post, any out-of-squareness is readily apparent on both members. Say the string touches the bottom corner of the post, but is 1/4" away from the top corner. This 1/4" offset must be marked on the brace. Likewise, the irregularities of the brace must be marked on the post. Because both pieces are not perfectly square, if you want a tight joint, their shoulders cannot be perfectly square either. By using the plumb bob to transfer each timber's unique irregularities to its mating member, the correct shoulder can be sawn to fit perfectly.

It was a beautiful thing to watch the French team teaching the bemused Americans this foreign method, in the same way that the Americans taught square-rule to their foreign friends. There was some jovial banter throughout the week about the merits of one or the other system, but in truth, this kind of cultural sharing is exactly what CSF aims for. And who can deny that the world is a more beautiful place when people of different perspectives share their vision of life? I was moved to see how this crew uses these projects to cultivate that very thing. They aren't called Carpenters "Without Borders" for nothing.

OPPOSITE: Léo Rousseau sights the plumb line along the plane of the post, marking the location with a pencil.

BELOW: Alicia Spence scribes a curved brace into the pentagonal ridge.

This cultural collaboration was just as obvious in the kitchen. Between Julia, Paula, and Grace (New Englanders), Lauren (an Italian from Philadelphia), Kinga (Polish), and Florence (French), a wide range of inspiration was brought to the table. There were mountains of veggies to chop, cauldrons of soups and stews to tend, and endless runs to the local farms for supplies. Feeding a total of 50 people three meals (and an afternoon snack) per day for 11 days is no small feat. For weeks after the event, Julia kept telling me about all of the tips she learned from the rest of the kitchen crew. Even just seeing the culinary variety opened her mind to tantalizing new ways to prepare dishes. Because Lauren runs her own catering business, she has a firm grasp of what it takes to feed crowds of people. She also brought some of her best recipes to contribute. Kinga and Florence have done several CSF projects before and they knew well the needs of the team, especially in light of the increase of caloric input needed to sustain intensive, manual labor. Kinga, in particular, had some good tips to keep the work running smoothly: baked goods at 3:30; lots of good coffee all the time; and bread, bread, and more bread. All day, every day, the kitchen at the other side of the property was just as busy as the carpentry site.

The provision of bread was actually something Julia and I particularly worried about in the early planning phases. We had heard how highly the French value their hearty loaves. What American in their right mind would feel confident offering bread to French guests? Even though we bake sourdough bread at home, we rarely make more than a few loaves a week – a fraction of what CSF would require. Fortunately, Kinga is a professional bread baker, and has been involved in several of the past projects to keep the gluten levels topped up. As we worked out the details of baking, we connected Kinga with Tim Semler and Lydia Moffet, who own a wood-fired bread company called Tinder Hearth just 10 minutes away. They graciously allowed Kinga access to the oven between their

bakes and their famous pizza nights (which are booked days in advance). Kinga determined that for this many people for this long, she would need to bake 80 loaves. When we told Tim this number, he laughed. "I love the French," he said, "For them, the bread *is* the meal." I can attest to this – 110 pounds of flour makes a lot of bread! Kinga's loaves were absolutely delicious and each required diligent surveillance at mealtime, lest it disappear too quickly. In fact, Kinga's bread has become such a staple for CSF projects that it was among the first things I heard about their work. I mean, what kind of self-respecting carpentry team doesn't bring their own baker?

"Traditional, intuitive bread making does not lend itself naturally to a written recipe. Before the study of microbiology, bakers understood the subtleties of the process. The nature of fermentation was second nature to their own. That is, they understood fermentation in relation to the rhythms of their own lives."

– Chad Robertson, *Tartine Bread*

As I write this, and I look out the window to the standing frame, I see a beautiful object, yes. But every carpenter knew from the beginning that this project wasn't ultimately about the frame at all – it was about people. In the big picture, this frame stands as a monument to the cultural exchange we shared this week. Everything from the variety of hewing patterns left behind (each as distinctive as the carpenter who made it), to the blending of joinery traditions, to the convergence of foodways that fueled the work, to the thoughtful (and sometimes hilarious) graffiti left on the ridge beam for my great-great grandchildren to discover someday, highlights the fact that this project was always about people. Nobody wants to travel across the world to be a cog in a machine. When we share burdens (whether emotional or physical), we share a bond, and handcraft is uniquely conducive to this kind of exchange. We could choose to design our work to serve the modern efficiency paradigm, but this inevitably leads to mechanization, mass-production, and specialization. It's when we resolve to slow down, to quiet ourselves before our work, that the spirit of sharing flourishes.

When I first arrived in the USA, many people taught me new slang words, such as "buddy." After saying it once or twice I began to mispronounce it as "beauty."

"Can you lend me your chisel, beauty?"

"That's a nice joint, beauty!"

"Can you come give me a hand, beauty?"

Everyone laughed, but nobody seemed to understand I was trying to say "buddy," until one day Blaine asked me, "Why are you always so flirty with me?" He finally explained to me that I was saying the wrong word. From that point on, everyone adopted the saying.

– Loïc Desmonts, *France*

I am sitting in a 70-year-old grove of gingkos at an arboretum near my home in Virginia. It is late autumn and the prehistoric trees are barren, yet aglow; uplit by the bed of once-golden leaves now amber-colored in their process of decay, decomposing into fertilizer for new growth. It is a cold, gray, and misty late-November day.

The quiet stillness I now experience juxtaposes sharply against my memory of the steady rhythm of axes chopping, scoring, hewing, and carving. With their cadence, our axes brought forth geometry and regularity out of the organic potential of the red and white pine logs.

Typically, timber framing workshops are focused on the teaching of unfamiliar skills by a handful of talented veterans to a group of emerging, interested carpenters, but the Carpenters Without Borders project was unique in that the crew was comprised almost entirely of an international group of professional timber framers. All of these men and women have spent years, decades, practicing and studying their craft and tools, and undoubtedly, any of them were capable of creating the building by themselves. Yet we chose to come together to freely give our time.

But why would a person do such a thing? Besides the fact that it is a carpenter's passion and joy to practice their craft, the opportunity to work with 30 international timber framers, doing hand-tool-only conversion and joinery, was a gift.

The age of the crew ranged amongst five decades, and while this was not a project directly focused on teaching, what made it so wonderful was that everyone came with such humility and enthusiasm to learn and to share. Even if conscious teaching moments were intermittent, learning was constant. We shared tools, techniques, stories, humor, sweat, blisters, meals, celebration, and general daily life. The depth of the conviviality and good spirits stemmed directly from our shared love of handcraft, "real" things, and the unbelievable (rare) graciousness of our hosts at *Mortise & Tenon Magazine* – Joshua, Julia, and Mike.

A large part of what made the experience so special for me was the opportunity to include Asher, my 12-year-old son, in the event. He has worked with me in the shop and on-site since he was five. He has grown up in the presence of many wonderful people that I've had the good fortune to work with. He can say, like Loïc Desmonts, who is now 21 and grew up working in his father's shop in France, "I was born in the wood chips." Projects like this have a formative impact on the lives of craftsmen and serve as milestones, pivot points in their careers, no matter what age. For many, it is a natural culmination of all they have worked for over many years. For other, younger carpenters, it serves as an awakening, a spring point and a confirmation of the possibility of what they yearn for, but may be unable to name or identify – the spiritual nourishment that comes from work worth doing.

Asher's knowledge, desire, and strength have only grown since he was a little boy. There is much that he has learned in working directly with me, but possibly even more has come from the community of builders that I've been blessed to associate with. In the first few days, we worked side-by-side, scoring, joggling, and hewing the round logs into square timbers. Later, he helped Loïc build the "goat" (tripod for the pitsaw) where he worked as both top dog and underdog to produce some of the curved braces. He worked with Gustave, a passionate and knowledgeable French carpenter, cutting joinery with only an axe. Towards the end, when we needed more pole rafter stock, Asher felled five red pine trees under the direction of the great woodswoman Alicia Spence, as I offered supervision and assistance. My heart leapt with pride and joy as I watched this young man harvest the trees with nothing more than an axe and his hands. We all look for potency, agency in the world, especially young people. I could see the confidence, reverence, and humility in his broad

smile as his blistered hands produced the crisp chopping which yielded the great whoosh of the tree top skimming the branches of its siblings just prior to coming to rest on the forest floor with a resounding, satisfying thud.

Asher learned so much from the dozens of adults who included him in this work, and while the end result of the building is the composite effort of so many individuals acting as one, he could reflect and know that his contribution was significant and real and lasting.

I can only say thank you so many times to all of those who so generously included him, but I say it again – thank you, especially Will, Hank, François, and Joshua. You have helped to plant a new tree and put an old head on a new axe handle. Just as we are indebted to our predecessors for putting forth this kind of work – showing us what is possible – so we have an obligation to share this with our young people. To give them real tools, real materials, and an appreciation for real work is our duty and, too often overlooked, logical end.

Someday, someone will ask our children, "Where did you learn to do this?" I hope they look back quizzically, perplexed by the reasoning of a mind that leads to such a question, and respond, "We've always done this. They gave these tools to us."

Who are the "they?" We must put tools in the hands of our children!

JORDAN FINCH, *USA*

CHAPTER 7

Camaraderie

"I'm very troubled by the amount of vicarious living we do, the time we spend watching someone else play ball or have adventures. . . . I see a time when all will recognize our need to feel useful and needed by the society around us – knowing that only through work, lovingly done, will come the growth and sense of belonging that are a part of mature adulthood."

William Coperthwaite – *A Handmade Life*

THURSDAY, AUGUST 29TH

Everything was ahead of schedule and going so smoothly that we welcomed the gentle rain that came on Thursday morning. I took half of the crew to visit Lie-Nielsen Toolworks, located about an hour-and-a-half south of us. Thomas Lie-Nielsen, always a gracious host, greeted us upon our arrival and treated us as his special guests. We were given a tour of the facilities and got to see all that goes into making their revered woodworking hand tools. Tom even showed us some test results of the new finishes he's trying on his handles – it felt like silk and was environmentally friendly. Tom's passion for quality was an inspiration to all of us. We ended the tour at the showroom, in which all of the Lie-Nielsen tools were available to play around with. The carpenters were so impressed that some couldn't stand to go home empty-handed. What is it that they say about investing in quality things? "You only cry once."

The other half of the crew that stayed back at the site that morning spent time under a tent chopping rafter mortises in the five-sided ridge beam and the step-lap notches in the plates. It was a delightful and calm morning of work – no one pushed too hard.

After we got back together in the afternoon, each team finished up the joinery for their assigned assembly. Those who were farther along jumped on the shaving horses to make more pegs, worked on the joists for the second floor, or shaved fresh surfaces on the rafters, which had developed a thin mildew after debarking. The team assigned to the ridge beam also spent time fitting the rafter tenons into their mortises.

"Who knows but if men constructed their dwellings with their own hands, and provided food for themselves and families simply and honestly enough, the poetic faculty would be universally developed, as birds universally sing when they are engaged? . . . Shall we forever resign the pleasure of construction to the carpenter?"

– Henry David Thoreau, *Walden*

Louis Jamin and Sophie Wintzer at the Lie-Nielsen Toolworks showroom.

The view of the worksite from the woodshop's second-floor windows was magical. I saw a swarm of busy workers set to their individual tasks, conscious that they were part of a team working toward a common goal. The workflow looked seamless as they got nearer and nearer to the finish line. I can't think of any other moment in the construction process that better exemplified the camaraderie in this team's work. Thursday afternoon's bird's-eye view of these final stages brought this home for me. The frame was nearly complete, and spirits were up, knowing we still had an entire work-day ahead of us to wrap things up before Saturday's raising.

We need the camaraderie of others. Although we might like to feel like we are autonomous beings who can make our own existence, not one of us does what we do without the help or inspiration of others. This is the flip side of the journey toward independence discussed in chapter five. Perhaps we'd be better to call it "interdependence."

Human beings were not designed to be solitary creatures. "Love" is a meaningless word without another upon whom you can bestow your affection. "Success" is empty when we have no one with whom we can share it. "Work" becomes drudgery when we lose sight of its ultimate purpose: namely, bettering the world in service to our neighbors.

Carpenters, 16th century. A 19th-century version based on an original 16th-century wood engraving. From *Le Moyen Age et la Renaissance*, by Paul Lacroix, Ferdinand Séré, and A. Rivaud, Volume III (Paris, 1849).

"The long buried seeds of a richer human culture… will draw freely on the compost from many previous cultures."

– Lewis Mumford, *The Pentagon of Power*

TRADITION AS CAMARADERIE

Our families, neighbors, and communities are the primary influences that shape us and make us who we are, and because of this, we are indebted to their wisdom and achievements. No one has taught themselves to hunt, or cook, or build – we all develop our thoughts and skills through direct instruction or by studying the works of others. Even the most revolutionary inventions were built on the discoveries and labors of the past. There is nothing new under the sun.

It has become common in postmodern culture to view tradition as an impersonal set of rules – arbitrary, rigid, and unbending. It is framed as if human history could be divided into two eras: all the unsophisticated generations before us, and the pinnacle of this present moment. We are led to believe that "they" (to use that all-encompassing word) used to believe or do certain things that we who "know better now" would never stoop to. This is a perspective that has been aptly described as "chronological snobbery." [14]

In fact, the decision to work within a tradition is a decision to collaborate with the labors of those who have gone on before – transgenerational camaraderie, if you will. We learn the best ways to make timbers square by studying the tool marks that reveal the ancient process. The tools we use today (whether they're electrified or not) are the development of thousands of years of artisanal practice. They work now because they worked then. We will, no doubt, continue to be sold this year's "groundbreaking" advances in technological equipment that will make obsolete everything that has come before. It is important that we as craftspeople especially push against this spirit of "snobbery" by embracing the understanding that tradition is "the accumulation of the experience and wisdom of many generations… an aggregate power that in all cases transcends the individuals." If we can assimilate this vision into our own creative works, we will find that the individual artisan is "able to produce work of astonishing merit with the utmost ease." [15]

As makers, we should continually work to cultivate the humility to hear what the past can teach us, because so many of us want our work to be lasting, sincere, and full of beauty. We want to make an impact in this world, to be able to stand back and appreciate the standing house, the delectable feast, or the freshly oiled landscape painting. This yearning exists within us, because we know deep down that our work matters. It matters for us, and it matters for our neighbors.

There is also an enrichment that comes by laboring with those of our own generation. Our friends and companions bring along with them experiences and skills that we cannot do without. And when our daily tasks are shared with others, there are innumerable opportunities for conversation and mutual support. Even in the silence of focus, another simply being there to support you carries the work on. This emotional bolstering is something that cannot be manufactured or synthesized. There is no technology that replaces our need for companionship. Our fractured and divided world needs the solidarity that blossoms out of experiences like shared labor.

The inclusion of French scribe carpentry on the UNESCO list of the Intangible Cultural Heritage of Humanity in 2009 is testimony to its long history and is in recognition of the tradition's strong internal culture with its own language and practices.

The UNESCO Intangible Cultural Heritage Convention aims to maintain the oral traditions, practices, and knowledge which we inherit from our ancestors. The transmission of these cultural practices and traditions to each successive generation is essential to human diversity. In the case of carpentry, it is not merely buildings or structures that the Convention intends to preserve, but the combination of cultural practices and physical structures of schools, which support the training and transmission of knowledge which underlies the practice of French scribe carpentry and in particular, the *trait de charpente*.

Among carpenters, knowledge is structured differently than in most contexts in modern 21st-century society. It is characterized by a cooperative spirit, which is inclusive and non-hierarchical. In carpentry training in France, along with many other trades and crafts, the habitual trope of the classroom teacher-pupil relationship, with its strict hierarchy of knowledge, is much less dominant than in the UK. Peer-to-peer learning is encouraged, if not the norm. Indeed, it plays an essential part in an apprentice's acquisition of trade knowledge. Problem-solving is both individual and collective.

Alongside the *Compagnonnage* and the technical colleges which are the core of France's carpentry training system, there exists also a strong subculture of independent carpenters, who in the terms of the *Compagnon* guilds are "*renards*" (foxes), that is, individuals who operate outside the rules and norms of the guild corporation.

Many individuals have become skilled carpenters by being autodidacts and by learning from and working with an entirely informal network of friends and colleagues. Experience is gained through *rendez-vous* gatherings or workshops. Participants come together to voluntarily and mutually assist in a community or similar project. Over a week or so, timbers are hewn and wrought into a finished building as the finer points of *lignage* or *piquage* are demonstrated, in an exchange of mutual learning.

The exceptional nature of the *Charpentiers Sans Frontières* meetings is also inspired by this free spirit of mutual learning, exchange, and knowledge transmission.

It has been my privilege to participate in several CSF projects, including the event hosted by Joshua and his *Mortise & Tenon* colleagues, as well as workshops organized by independent carpenters in France. The range of cultural diversity; the dissolution of the habitual social frontiers of gender, age, and nationality; and the opening of otherwise-rare avenues of communication all make for a small revolution in a world normally regulated by an excess of constraints.

Many of the putative benefits of modernity have come at a great cost to the human spirit. The commodification of knowledge benefits only a tiny minority of the population and serves to create hierarchies which divide and diminish the rest of us. I am convinced that one of the ways humanity must remake itself in the light of the many problems we face is to re-establish those lost connections which have now left us divided and diminished. Rehumanizing knowledge is an essential part of this, and the practice of carpentry in a spirit of infinitely open exchange and communication is one small way to do this.

ANDY HYDE, *UK*

Early on in the week, Mike and I washed most of the dishes. After each meal, every plate, bowl, glass, and utensil was washed by either him or me. At this quantity, along with all of our other responsibilities, we quickly fell behind. The workload was more than we could manage before the next meal. After a couple days of constant frenzy, the team graciously offered to pitch in. At each morning meeting, Will G. asked for three volunteers to take up the task of doing dishes. Everyone was eager to help, and it made an enormous difference to Mike and me.

Because I am a stubborn and independent person, it is humbling to receive help like this. Especially as the host, being brought beyond my capacity was a merciful reminder that I need others. (I've learned this many times in my life, and every time I do, I remember that I've learned this many times in my life. I am still a work in process.)

While it is true that "many hands make light work," it's even more important to realize that a unified team is greater than the sum of its parts. As we prepared for this project during the *M&T* summer workshop, our six students completed more in two days than Mike and I could have done in weeks. Besides setting the granite foundation blocks, we weeded and mulched my garden and chopped mortises for a floor system in my barn. But as we accomplished a mountain of work over those two days, it felt more like play because of the conviviality of shared experience.

It is possible to learn to log with horses; and hew your own timbers with an axe; and design, join, and even raise (with clever devices or heavy machinery) a frame all by yourself. You'd be able to tell everyone how amazing you are to accomplish the build without the help of another soul. But what's the fun in that? I've always enjoyed quiet shop time as much as any other woodworker, but from the projects I've done with other people (such as finishing off the woodshop, building workbenches, or chairmaking), I realize solitude is not nearly as fun as comradeship.

If you're used to working alone, try this for yourself: Invite your friends into your shop. Woodworkers love to hang out and talk tools. Invite that co-worker who has expressed interest in woodworking but never seems to know how to take the plunge. Make disciples of the craft. Hand work is infectious, and usually, it only takes one completed project for another life-long maker to be born into the world.

CHAPTER 8
Gathering the World

"The culture of the table [allows us to center our lives] by joining simplicity with cosmic wealth. . . . [An earthen jug] teaches us what it is to hold, to offer, to pour, and to give. In its clay, it gathers for us the earth as it does in containing the wine that has grown from the soil. It gathers the sky whose rain and sun are present in the wine. It refreshes and animates us in our mortality. And in the libation it acknowledges and calls on the divinities. . . . Truly human eating is the union of the primal and the cosmic. In the simplicity of bread and wine, of meat and vegetable, the world is gathered."

Albert Borgmann — *Technology and the Character of Contemporary Life*

FRIDAY, AUGUST 30TH

Friday on the jobsite was all about finishing the remaining joinery and cleaning up in preparation for Saturday's raising. Tools were gathered, scattered drinking glasses were recovered, and load after load of wood chips were piled into wheelbarrows and consolidated into one mound at the bottom of the field. (Mike and I intend to turn this into a *hügelkultur* garden in the coming year.)

As a collaboration, Victor Calame and Louis Jamin designed and carved a delightful image of a carpenter hewing with a French axe right above the doorway. The drawing was flanked with "CsF" and "2019" to commemorate the event. On this day also, Scottish spoon carver Paul Cookson carved the decorative ram's-head wedge that would be used to lock the through tenon of the king post at the raising.

Because there was extra time on this day, several folks decided to decorate the rafter tails with carving. Paul Cookson took the lead. He went around gathering symbols and logos that carried special significance to members of the team, and once these were decided, every one of the 24 rafter tails was carved. Those symbols of our friendship will remain long after we are gone.

That evening we had a celebratory lobster feast on Pumpkin Island at the kind invitation of the owners, George and Dawn. Pumpkin Island is located in Eggemoggin Reach, and retains a lighthouse that was in operation between 1854 and 1933. Our time out there was a beautiful punctuation to the work that had been accomplished during the week. Several members from the foreign team had never eaten a lobster before and were excited to try. It was hilarious fun teaching our guests how to eat these sea bugs. Some of our more enthusiastic carpenters (not saying any names, Léo) got pretty wet with lobster juice. We all had lighthearted, silly fun – a refreshing calm before the big day.

The *Traverivera*

One evening when we were all sitting around the table drinking together, I had the idea to teach everyone to play the *Traverivera*, which is a singing game. It goes, "Do you know how to sing the *Traverivera*? Do you know how to pass this bottle without making an error?" While you sing, everyone has to tap their glass on the table, then pass it to their neighbor on the right, keeping the beat of the song, but remembering to stop at the last phrase. I had never played with so many people, and it was hilarious watching everyone mess up, one after another. After that night, I heard carpenters singing the *Traverivera* on the jobsite.

– Loïc Desmonts, *France*

Janne Aikonen carving a personal symbol on one of the rafter tails.

In fact, every one of our evenings was full of sharing and fun – either a local tour or slideshow presentation from one of the carpenters. François makes sure to include these talks at every CSF project, and it is a unique opportunity to learn about minutiae you don't hear about anywhere else. We had many different presenters: Gustave Rémon talked about French axes throughout medieval history, François covered the recent fire tragedy at Notre Dame, Alicia Spence explained the preservation of the African House in Louisiana, Andres Uus showed several of his conservation projects around Europe, Carlos Barbero showed the restoration of a water wheel, and I shared our vision at *Mortise & Tenon Magazine*. These presentations gave us an even greater appreciation for the skill present in the group.

Alongside the amazing amount of work that was accomplished, we also had time for a few evening tours. Early in the week, we caravanned down to the Deer Isle Hostel, to meet with Dennis Carter who showed us around his timber frames and gardens. It's always inspiring to visit Dennis and his partner, Anneli, to check out their sprawling off-grid homestead with extensive gardens and more and more accommodations all the time. Besides the timber frames, Dennis wanted to show us all of the different uses of wood on their homestead,

including water-retention mulch in the garden, sawdust for the compost bucket toilets, and wood-chip mulch to heat the water for their outdoor shower. Dennis and Anneli are perhaps the closest thing to self-sufficiency I've known. Dennis told me the story about when he was just about finished building the hostel and needed to construct staging brackets on the second story to install the roof. He ran to the hardware store for some lag bolts. It was at that point that he realized this was the first trip to the store he made in the whole project. The total for that hardware store run was $16.

Later on in the week, my friends Damian and Amy came over to talk about the 1720s Massachusetts house they resurrected and restored on their property. After a brief slideshow of the historic record and dismantling, we all went over to their place for a tour. The carpenters were all over the place, analyzing every nook and cranny. There was much discussion about the timber markings and joinery styles. Damian said he's never had any guests over that were this into the details of the frame. They both looked surprised but excited to watch 40 enthusiastic wood nerds crawling all around their house with flashlights. Let this be a lesson to us: Be careful what kind of people you invite over!

OPPOSITE: Gustave Rémon presents his research in historic French axe patterns after dinner.

ABOVE: Dennis Carter shows us around the Deer Isle Hostel.

LEFT: The carpenters examining Damian and Amy's 1720s house.

Looking forward to CSF, I was stunned by the sheer immensity of cooking. Our small home was turned inside-out to accommodate bushels of food, and after the project's inertia took over, my task became providing the constant flow of raw ingredients and space for creativity to blossom.

The daily connections with farmers deepened our bond as they rejoiced to see their lovingly produced food fueling the builders. During many a post-lunch meeting to discuss the plan for the next day's meals, Kinga and I choked back tears at the weight of the task. But without fail, upon returning to the kitchen, each day brought us an army of fresh helpers ready to wash, peel, and chop. These volunteers came to participate in and support the magic. It was the energy of our joyful conversations that carried the communal work.

My dear friend, Lauren, came early to start the engine of meal creation for the week. She flew in from Philadelphia bringing with her endless energy, characteristic Italian love, and the joy of preparing food for people. Her wit and humor filled our days with side-splitting laughter as pots, pans, and ingredients flew. And as if by magic, meal after meal appeared out of the hilarity from the light of dawn to the deep of the night.

This scale of cooking demanded ingenuity, especially in light of our priorities to waste nothing and to match the meals with the mood and weather of the day. Kinga, whose creativity extends beyond bread, and Florence, with French inspiration for showcasing flavors directly from the garden, whipped out platters of glowing produce paired perfectly with their seasonings (fresh mayonnaise to die for) in the final moments before each meal. "Ditch the menu," "Use what you have," "Waste nothing" were the guiding principles here, and delicious creativity abounded. I made vain attempts to procure roots of parsley and celery for a Polish borscht, but creativity carried us on. It was in Kinga's encouragement to reinterpret the goat cheese I had proclaimed a failure that I sensed the disparity between my own culture of waste and overconsumption and this foreign spirit of spontaneity and innovation, to use every scrap of wholesomeness, discarding nothing. From second-hand dishes, linens, and water coolers, to cooking from scratch and cleaning and maintaining reusables, "waste nothing" became our anthem.

And it was a cauldron of chili that brought our native cooking instincts together in creative climax. We gathered 'round, five cooks from different traditions: French, Polish, Philadelphia Italian, Maine foodie, and Southern cookin' origins, lending our taste buds and ideas. "Wait. Cocoa powder in the chili? Are you sure?" But Kinga's surprising addition turned out to be the perfect touch. Only when these hands reached across borders, languages, and measuring systems did such an unexpected masterpiece emerge.

An atmosphere of gratitude sweetened the daily exchanges between cooks and carpenters. Each took pause to savor the fruits of our labor. And they continually implored us frenzied Americans to sit with them to enjoy the moment. Even as they wolfishly scarfed the meals (inspiring Kinga's hawk-like monitoring of portions), they shared their appreciation of the food's freshness and the kitchen's care, and reminded us that it is wholesome food that fuels their work. It's a lesson I carry with me now: to pause and notice food and the process involved in bringing it from the earth to the table. Woven through the week was deep respect for the earth and its bounty across cultures, ages, and languages. Food of joy is possible, and magic is created in the process.

JULIA KLEIN, *USA*

SHARING MEALS

Being able to treat our guests to local culture is something that we set out to do from the beginning. We knew they were traveling far and long, and many of them had never been to the United States before, so we were determined to share our home with them as much as possible. A major part of this welcome was sharing our community's food – almost all of it from our friends, who are farmers, or our town's thriving food co-operative. As a way to express our gratitude to the carpenters, we determined to return the joy of a new building with "the long celebrated joys of sharing food grown by local hands from local lands." [16]

The value of sourcing food close to home goes beyond a goal of recommended nutritional balance or optimal flavor (though absolutely everything was wholesome and delicious). The most basic reason this was important was because it was a way we could give of ourselves. There was no way we could bring ourselves to outsource this most basic gesture of appreciation. Throughout the week, the carpenters told us often how much it meant to them that we regarded doing the food ourselves as an essential component of the success of this project.

The importance of sharing a meal made from scratch was emphasized in philosopher Albert Borgmann's book, *Technology and the Character of Contemporary Life*. Borgmann explores the value of engagement with the world through disciplined practices, such as learning to play an instrument, running outdoors, or what he calls "the culture of the table" over against the disabling nature of the technological paradigm.

What does it take to feed 35 hungry carpenters?

Set menu to blend cultural and dietary preferences.
Raise and process chickens.
Connect with local farmers and producers.
Organize kitchen and transform house for mass food production.
Stock pantry and fill freezer with meat.
Order and receive produce.
Connect with friends who will bring meals and help.
Prep each meal a day or two ahead.
Adjust menu each day for incoming produce and using leftovers.
Chop, chop, and cook, panic a little, chop and cook some more.
Fill out meals with last-minute inspirations from farm and garden.
Schlep meal to the shop and arrange for the hungry crew.
Ring the dinner bell!
Oversee the feasting to make sure everyone gets their fair share.
Clean up and wash.
Do it all over again, but always with the help of friends.

– Julia Klein

Donna and Andy Birdsall of Horsepower Farm harvest potatoes at the end of the season.

This "culture of the table" is proffered as a prime example of an activity that supports increasing awareness and appreciation of the world because it is about more than simply good food; it is an expansive concept that includes the "delectable things nature has brought forth," the farmer that grew them, the cook, food customs or traditions, and family and friends that feast together, in one interconnected web. Borgmann tells us that "the preparation of food draws near the harvesting and the raising of the vegetables in the garden close by. This context of activities is embodied in persons. The dish and the cook, the vegetable and the gardener tell of one another." It is important to remember that all food has its origin in the soil, whether it has been a plant rooted in the garden or an animal grazing the nourishment of the fields. Local farmers Phil and Heather Retberg have put it succinctly: "All flesh is grass. All grass is soil." Seen in this holistic way, the kitchen becomes an extension of the garden. Its job is to convey that abundance to the counter, the pot, and the table. Will Lisak reflected during the week, "There's something rewarding about being involved with the processing of your food; preparing the meal is just as enjoyable as the meal itself."

The joy of feeding others is an act of service rooted so deeply within us that Borgmann describes it as "one of the most generous gestures human beings are capable of." The recipient, in exchange, is called upon to cultivate a "respectful and skilled response to the great things that are coming to pass in the meal." By this Borgmann means, I think, that we meaningfully engage with our loved ones in the process of eating when we learn to identify and appreciate the "great things" of mutual love and openness that we experience through meals made with affection. When this happens, eating becomes feasting. "What seems to be a mere receiving and consuming of food is in fact the enactment of generosity and gratitude."

The conviviality of sharing a meal creates an opportunity for meaningful conversation that might otherwise be left unexplored in the frenzy of contemporary life. It is a time to embrace, a time to ponder and wonder and deliberate together. The cooks, seated in the midst, are thanked and praised. And a toast is made for more moments like these. "In the preparation of a meal we have enjoyed the simple tasks of washing leaves and cutting bread; we have felt the force and generosity of being served a good wine and homemade bread. . . . In the simplicity of bread and wine, of meat and vegetable, the world is gathered."

This simplicity of communal eating is a profoundly human thing, and like swinging an axe with a friend, enriches our experience of life. It is something that is available to us each day, if we will only make the time for it. Borgmann tells us that "it is within our power to clear a central space amid the clutter and distraction [of our lives]. We can begin with the simplicity of a meal that has a beginning, a middle, and an end and that breaks through the superficiality of convenience food in the simple steps of beginning with raw ingredients, preparing and transforming them, and bringing them to the table. In this way we can again become freeholders of our culture." [17]

I've tried on many occasions to relate to polite inquirers and curious friends something of the heart of the CSF blacksmith shop project.

–

Every time, I've failed miserably.

How can you briefly summarize an experience so powerfully novel, so exhaustingly exhilarating, so beautifully redefining of what you thought possible, without descending into meaningless, blubbering superlatives?

You can't. At least, as you can see, I can't.

So I've taken to sharing snapshots from the week of the project – moments frozen in memory that stir the potent awe that still lingers in my mind, like the dust that hangs in the air after a big tree falls.

As one of the countless preparations leading up to the event, I built a long temporary worktable across the back of our shop so that the carpenters could keep their tools up off the ground during mealtimes. When Hank and Will showed up a few days early, the two of them alone filled that surface to overflowing, with just their own tools they'd hauled in. Uh, these guys were serious. I built more tables.

On the night the European team arrived, I drove a 12-passenger van loaded with carpenters and gear from the bus station to the houses where they'd be staying for the duration. It was over an hour's drive, and Florian and I talked most of the way. Answering his questions about local history, ecology, and how cold it gets in winter renewed my perception about what a special place Maine is. It's a wonderful gift to look at your home with fresh eyes.

I tried to not let my mouth hang open too dumbly as I watched Gustave trim 1/2" off the end of a big tenon using only his axe. He executed the operation perfectly, more neatly and quickly than I would likely do with a saw.

There were a number of such moments throughout the week, many involving incredibly skilled work accomplished with an axe alone. This tool can do anything.

There was that evening on Pumpkin Island, after the food was eaten and the sunset was long past, when the last of us were being ferried back to Little Deer Isle in groups of five or six. We sat on the float at the end of the dock, watching the spotlight of Scott's workboat fade into the distance across the harbor. Songs were sung, jokes were told under the stars. I found an oar and stirred up the phosphorescent algae from the cold depths, and we all shared a moment of silent awe – the Milky Way was both above us and beneath us.

On raising day, when the last of the rafters were going up, I was scuttling around with the video camera trying to capture the details of the operation. A man, a visitor from nearby, had been quietly contemplating the scene for some time from a good vantage point beneath a pine tree. I'd moved that way and began setting up the tripod when he spoke, obviously quite moved. "It's just so beautiful. All of it," he said.

I couldn't agree more.

MICHAEL UPDEGRAFF, *USA*

Many hands from different countries joined together for a week to create a traditional handmade timber-framed structure. Upon arrival, hands reached across cultural boundaries to greet with salutations and smiles.

We all knew what we were here to do, and we eagerly found our places to create among strangers who were to become friends.

Hand-drawn plans of the structure we were creating, rendered in advance, were put on view to give details, and steer us to our ultimate goal of building a blacksmith's shop.

Benches and sawhorses were placed to hold tools and timbers.

Hands guided axes to hew, producing a distinctive, rhythmic, and grounding sound as the blade connected with the log, over and over, resulting in a rectilinear, smooth-faced timber and producing a bed of chips that softened our footfalls. Hands grasped the handles of saws as teeth spat out sawdust and kerfs were created, sometimes with one hand, sometimes with four.

Trees were felled from the forest, gripping axes, a subtle twist of the wrist guiding the intended point of the strike.

Hands taught other hands how and where to hold an axe, how to guide the blade of a plane to create a transparent sliver of wood, how to create a smooth face using the bevel of a chisel, how to scribe two faces of wood to join together almost imperceptibly, how to carve a spoon, how to make a peg using a drawknife, that would tie together and hold fast the structure.

Soon, hands were taped in protective patterns hoping to ward off the evil blister monster.

Many hands lovingly kneaded bread and cooked and created wonderful food to nourish our bodies for the work that we were all doing.

Hands moved through the water propelling bodies forward or grasped gunwales as we all made our way to an island to celebrate. Hands cracked open crustaceans, pulled out the meat and guided it to our mouths for our taste buds to explode and savor.

Pulses quickened and energy heightened as things came into place and were prepared for raising day. As each timber was finished, many hands hoisted and carried them to check their fit. Mortises, tenons, shoulders, and pegs were eased and worked until the elements of the corresponding joinery came together.

The morning of raising day, all pieces set in place, carpenters gathered to orchestrate the outline of the day. A check-in, a walkthrough of the process before us and the continual reminder to be safe.

The community converged to watch something they may never have seen; a hand-hewn timber frame, put together and raised completely by all the many hands that were responsible for its creation.

Bents are put together as our hands, so familiar at this point with the feel of these timbers, start to raise and bring the frame vertical. Connecting girts and knee braces come into play giving the frame its dimensional form. Rafter plates are parbuckled up the sides of the structure to seat mortises onto brace and post top tenons. A temporary upper floor is placed and scaffolding is erected. All joints are checked for final pegging.

Food, rest, water, breathe.

Building proceeds. Fiddlers show up to serenade us while we work. Tie beams, king posts, braces, ridge beam, and finally rafters are lifted into place, creating the plane of the roof. This gives the frame its form in the landscape. It is topped and grounded in the place that it will stand for a long, long time.

Finishing touches – rafter pegs pounded into place by family, peak crowned with a whetting bough, hand-carved ram's-horn wedge driven to hold the king post and symbolize the work of the carpenters, and a spoon peg added for discovery and whimsey.

Games, celebration, music, and dance.

Hands held glasses as we raised them to toast the history and tradition of our craft, our tired bodies, our camaraderie, our work, and the magic that enabled us to all be together doing what we love, grateful for the trees, our tools, and each other. A structure created by many hands in honor of an age-old tradition.

Hands, along with arms, gave deep parting hugs as we all went back out into the world, tired, but filled to the brim, knowing that we had created something beautiful, not only in structure, but in our hearts.

LIZABETH MONIZ, *USA*

CHAPTER 9
Raising a Monument

"Come muster, my lads, your mechanical tools,
Your saws and your axes, your hammers and rules.
Bring your mallets and planes, your level and line,
And plenty of pins of American pine…"

John Grigg — "The Raising" (1836)

SATURDAY, AUGUST 31ST

Saturday was the big raising day, and we invited the public to come watch the momentous occasion. Will Gusakov started the morning meeting by calmly explaining the importance of safety and attentiveness. He laid out the raising plan so that everyone understood. The crew was intent and ready to go. But there were so many carpenters available to help that we all had to wait our turn – too many people on the deck would become dangerous.

First, the west bent was assembled and raised. The raising crew was divided into three teams: the lifting, the pike poles, and the ropes to restrain the bent from overextending. At Will's confident direction, this first bent was lifted off the deck and overhead, at which point the pike poles engaged the tie beam to continue the thrust upwards. Once the bent was vertical, Vermont framer Miles Jenness used the commander (which is essentially a massive mallet) to steer the posts' bottom tenons into their mortises. When the posts dropped into place, the assembly was secured with temporary diagonal bracing to remain plumb.

Once the remaining two bents were up, connected to each other with horizontal timbers called "girts," and the frame began to take shape, I was overcome with emotion. It was paradoxical, because time seemed to stand still and slip away simultaneously. I don't know how else to describe it.

The house-builder at work in cities or anywhere,
The preparatory jointing, squaring, sawing, mortising,
The hoist-up of beams, the push of them in their places, laying
          them regular,
Setting the studs by their tenons in the mortises according as they
          were prepared,
The blows of mallets and hammers, the attitudes of the men,
          their curv'd limbs,
Bending, standing, astride the beams, driving in pins, holding on
          by posts and braces,
The hook'd arm over the plate, the other arm wielding the axe…

– Walt Whitman, "Song of the Broad-Axe"

The team was focused and attentive to Will G.'s instructions on the morning of the raising.

LEFT: The third bent is raised into place.

TOP: The second bent is assembled, ready to join the final bent.

BOTTOM: Will G. and Hank plumb the post.

It was similar to other momentous events in my life that I had long awaited or worked so hard to reach – my wedding, the births of my children, the raising of my woodshop. Just as I felt in those other instances, when this frame began to rise, I wanted time to slow. But it wouldn't. Each moment passed one after another, and all I could do was embrace and absorb every ounce of it before it was gone.

I keenly felt the tension between staying focused to do what needed to be done and wishing desperately we weren't approaching the end. Watching each step was as exciting as it was bittersweet.

When all three bents were joined and plumbness was confirmed, the girts' pegs were driven to tie the whole frame together. Temporary bracing was also fastened at the tops of the posts to maintain the correct spacing between the top tenons.

The next step was to lift the log joists into place. These joists dropped into mortises in the tie beams, and the flat hewed on their top sides created a flat plane that was even with the tops of the tie beams to apply flooring. Spruce subfloor, 2" thick, was temporarily fastened in place on the second level in order to continue raising the plates and roof structure.

The plates were lifted with ropes by a team above, a method called "parbuckling" (seen opposite). By tying several ropes at the top of the frame and laying the timber across them, the team above was able to hoist the free ends of the ropes to raise the beam. Each plate calmly, steadily rolled its way up the wall without struggle or serious hang-up. A final tap of the commander brought a confident "thunk" from the plates as they dropped down, fully engaging onto the tenons. The lifting of such a large member without machinery (or even the advantage of a gin pole) was an amazing thing to watch. With the help of friends, the simplest solutions are the best.

Carlos Barbero guides a
log joist up to the second level.

Right before lunch, the team began the first step of the roof assembly – raising the west gable post with its large curved braces. The final shape of the frame could almost be seen at this point. After a well-deserved midday feast, the entire team encircled the frame (whether they were actively on duty or not) to watch the building make it through to completion. The two remaining ridge posts were erected and braced, and the pentagonal ridge was set atop, in finicky coordination with its four diagonal braces beneath. After a bit of jostling, the ridge was set in place, and the only pieces left were the rafters. These half-round log rafters were handed up one by one to the team on the second floor. Their tenons were slid into the ridge mortises and pegged, and the tails were lowered into the step laps cut in the plates.

The ritual driving of the final pegs and king post wedge were special moments to behold. For these last parts, we disassembled the rope barrier around the site, and invited the public to share in this moment with us. The CSF team saved the honors of driving the king post wedge, the pegs in the rafter tails, and the center post's ridge tenon for François and those who helped with all of the food, housing, and other details. The installation of these last elements is quite ceremonial and affords a special opportunity for expressions of gratitude and appreciation.

First, François drove the ram's-horn wedge, which was carved by Paul Cookson. François spoke humbly about his unsuitability for this honor and thanked everyone for working, feasting, and fellowshipping with such passion and kindness.

Before the final rafters were pegged, Will Gusakov gave a brief speech to the crowd gathered below. He expressed gratitude for the spirit and hard work of the team, including those who were in the kitchen and running errands. He talked about the historic symbolism of driving the final pegs and nailing the whetting bush (a ceremonial evergreen bough that honors the trees that were harvested for the frame) to the gable end of the ridge. As Will spoke, tears began to roll down his cheeks. Many of us were overcome with emotion and felt privileged to be a part of an experience so unique and special.

Florence, Grace, Paula, Kinga, Mike, and Scott proceeded to drive the rafter pegs, one by one. Every peg closer to completion elicited applause and excitement. Based on centuries-long tradition, Will decided that the final two pegs would be driven by Julia and me, the custodians of the newly birthed

Julia's father, Scott Pusey, drives a peg into the rafter tail.

frame. Before we did, however, Will explained to the crowd that the French tradition is that the owner's wife drove the final peg and the number of blows it took to drive it home determined the number of beers the owners had to buy for the crew! Even though we all had a good laugh, I heard several thirsty carpenters counting the blows out loud, "ONE, TWO, THREE…" It turned out that Julia was given a generously sized peg that took many blows to drive home, but with determination, she finally got it. The very last peg was my responsibility and the anticipation was high. I started the peg in the hole, and comically, mine was one of the slightest in the bunch, and slipped in with barely a tap! Laughter and cheers erupted in the crowd, and hugs were shared all around. As a final touch, Asher Finch, the youngest of the crew, nailed on the whetting bush under the proud watch of his father, Jordan.

ABOVE: Will Lisak shows us how to play "slack'em."

RIGHT: Miles Jenness delivers the beverages.

With the frame complete, the festivities began and continued long into the night – libations all around! The carpenters played various games including "slack'em," which is between two players, each standing on a half-round of a log. The objective is to either pull the long length of rope from your opponent's hand or cause them to fall off-balance and touch the ground. In addition to slack'em, we played a sort of "king of the hill" game in which a board was laid across two sawhorses, and two carpenters tried to hold balance while pushing the other off the board. We had ridiculous fun. I enjoyed seeing these carpenters completely carefree in contrast to the focused work of the prior nine days. Focus is certainly a healthy discipline, but sometimes it just feels good to shove someone off a plank.

After a big feast, a local fiddle band arrived to lead us in contra dances in the woodshop. There was a lot of sweaty stomping and hollering 'round-and-'round and up-and-down on that shop floor. We dosey-doed our partners for a good long while, until François asked to say a few words. He expressed his appreciation for our week together.

He talked about the bonds we now share across the borders of our countries. He also explained that our axes are symbolic weapons of mass "construction" – the building of the frame being a monument to the building of our deep friendship and shared conviviality. Then he presented me with a restored 19th-century French hewing axe as a token of our friendship – a generous gift that I will always cherish. We look forward to using this axe to work side-by-side with others for many years to come.

It was hard to go to bed that night, but even harder to say "goodbye" in the morning. Mike and I drove the foreign crew up to Bangor, vowing we would see each other again, but next time in *their* homes.

One of the carpenters, Alicia Spence, left a signed note for everyone that so beautifully summed up the feeling we shared: "Rather than saying 'Goodbye,' Let's say 'See you soon.' Travel safe, my friends. Where to? What's next?"

Being part of Charpentiers Sans Frontières is one of the great gifts this life has given me. Travel the world in great company, build beautiful structures with your hands — that's all wonderful, but to be able to toil alongside and learn from such dedicated craftsmen, and to exchange tools, skills, terminology, and approaches is the real gift.

At the 2018 bridge reconstruction in Harcourt, after each meal, the paper tablecloths were covered in pencil drawings of trusses, axe profiles, and joinery details. We had 13 nationalities represented that year, and everyone was curious to learn how the person sitting beside him would cut a particular joint or what tool they commonly used for a given task. The same spirit of camaraderie was present in Maine.

When we had just finished raising the frame for *Mortise & Tenon*, Joshua and Julia were given the task of driving the final pegs. I stood on the second-floor joists behind my friend Will Gusakov, as he explained to the crowd below that the French carpenters have a tradition of offering the lady of the house the honor of driving the last peg and she, in return,

will grant the crew one drink for every blow of the mallet required to send the peg home. Will and I had spent months planning this gathering as the stateside members of CSF. Months of correspondence with Joshua and Mike, and on a different schedule and sometimes in another language, with François and the rest of the European crew. Will is generally very focused and businesslike on site, and those traits had been amplified as he had been leading the raising, so I was surprised to hear his voice crack and falter as he started crying. But we were all overtaken with emotion up there, and there was hardly a dry eye.

When our friends left to return home the following morning, I couldn't keep it together either. It was hugging my friend Louis that did me in, but I even cried saying bon voyage to Gustave of all people! I'm kidding. Seeing the whole crew arrive at the start of the workshop, I felt like my family had been reunited, and now we were all heading our separate ways for another year. As I said on the night of the raising, when we were gathered to offer words of thanks to each other: We used to be born into a tribe, and had to find our individuality. Today we are born individuals, and need to find our tribe.

When I think back on the project, my mind doesn't conjure a specific log, joint, or frame detail. What I think of is the camaraderie, shared jokes, and the songs. It was a massive communal effort – in terms of logistics, planning, meals, and of course physical labor. While the task at hand is why we are there in the first place – to throw our minds and bodies into the work – our species has a knack for turning communal toil into joyful work.

HANK SILVER, *USA*

Truly Human Work

"We need to discover an alternative way of being-in-the-world that enables us to know and to make in such a way that created nature – including other people and, indeed, ourselves – is enabled to become more and not less of itself by virtue of our interaction with it."

Craig M. Gay – *Modern Technology and the Human Future*

This project has given a glimpse into an alternative economy, but it is not an economy in the sense of monetary exchange, nor that of looking for the least expensive way to build something. My use of the word "economy" here is instead a reference to the original Greek οικονομία (oikonomia) – an orientation and management of personal life. Wendell Berry has explained the important distinction between "economics" (the "study of money making") and "economy," which he describes as "the ways of human housekeeping, the ways by which the human household is situated and maintained within the household of nature… which is to say, in nature and in work." [18] This distinction is vital, Berry reminds us, because a carefully designed economy preserves "coherence or meaning in our lives."

This particular project, in its scale and intensity, is likely beyond the needs of most people – not everyone will host a team of French carpenters to build a blacksmith shop. There are no longer horse loggers in every community, not everyone owns a plot of harvestable trees, and the congestion of urban life may preclude large-scale hewing operations.

Everyone's circumstances are unique, and there are constraints intrinsic to each of them. If you've made a choice to maintain a stable career, it often means you've made a commitment to a particular geographical place. The joys of raising a family only come through relinquishing the autonomy of the single life. We all make choices. We pursue the things that are important to us, whether it be job, leisure, comfort, or family. Life is always an exercise in creating space for the things that we want to see flourish and grow.

But there are many things that can become possible for us, if only we are willing to make hard decisions and step out into the hope of something different. To succeed, we must hold the value of reaching our goals above the discomfort or inconveniences that we may experience along the way. Although we all find ourselves in different life circumstances in pursuit of a variety of aims, it is important to realize that our options are never limited solely to the consumption of industrially supplied commodities; *Charpentiers Sans Frontières* has shown us that something else is possible.

The beauty of a hewn frame is that the marks of the craftsperson will always remain.

Perhaps the thing that is possible for you is harvesting a tree branch to carve a spoon which you will bring to your cafeteria lunch. Maybe instead, you are inspired to fill a chest with hand tools and to designate a corner of your garage as shop space in which you learn to build furniture. Or it might be that this story has been the tiny spark that ignites a radical life change, a turning from the hustle of the city toward the woods to build a house with your own two hands. Surely, not many will choose such an extreme path, and not all are able. But even the smallest steps are movements toward engaged, humane living in an increasingly disengaged world.

What would our world look like if more people embraced
this kind of reconnection?

What will it look like in *your* life?

"The point is not simply that we have lost a kind of natural simplicity or innocence to which we must now strive somehow to return. Rather, what has been lost, as we have stressed repeatedly, is the possibility of encountering something outside ourselves that might direct and discipline – and thus give order to – human making and willing. In the absence of such discipline, modern machine technology appears destined to become more automatic, increasingly autonomous, and progressively removed from the needs and requirements of ordinary embodied human beings.

"So what is to be done? The short answer is we need a change of mind, a change of outlook. We need to discover a new way of seeing the world or, perhaps more to the point, of *attending* to it that doesn't simply 'enframe' the world as stuff to be put to use. We need to discover an alternative way of being-in-the-world that enables us to know and to make in such a way that created nature – including other people and, indeed, ourselves – is enabled to become more and not less of itself by virtue of our interaction with it. We need to reimagine our place and task in the world, furthermore, such that we might grow into that truly human vocation of caring for each other, for ourselves, and for created nature; of becoming, as Heidegger once put it, the 'shepherds of being.'"

– Craig M. Gay, *Modern Technology and the Human Future*

Illustration: Elizabeth Bennett

ENDNOTES

1. Peter Forbes, *A Man Apart: Bill Coperthwaite's Radical Experiment in Living* (White River Junction, VT: Chelsea Green Publishing, 2015), 192.

2. Nicholas Carr, *The Glass Cage: Automation and Us* (New York: W.W. Norton & Company, Inc., 2014), 149-150.

3. Isabelle Khurshudyan, "Nats have their wood bat preferences, but science suggests there is no difference," *Washington Post* (July 25, 2014), accessed December 11, 2019, https://www.washington-post.com/sports/nationals/nats- have-their-wood-bat-preferences-but-science-suggests-there-is-no-difference/2014/07/25/c8145624-01e9-11e4-b8ff-89afd3fad6bd_story.html.

4. I am indebted to philosopher Albert Borgmann for these insights and analysis. For more about the "device paradigm" see Albert Borgmann, *Technology and the Character of Contemporary Life* (Chicago: University of Chicago Press, 1984).

5. Mihaly Csikszentmihalyi, *Flow: The Psychology of Optimal Experience* (New York: HarperCollins Publishers, 1990).

6. Wendell Berry, *What Are People For?* (New York: North Point Press, 1990), 140.

7. Richard B. Gregg, *The Power of Nonviolence* (New York: Schocken Books, 1966), 168-169.

8. Quoted from Mahatma Gandhi, *Hind Swaraj and Other Writings* (Cambridge: Cambridge University Press, 1997), 168; and *The Collected Works of Mahatma Gandhi* (New Delhi: Publications Division Government of India, 1999), HTML electronic book, CWMG 53:1.

9. John Spargo, *Syndicalism, Industrial Unionism and Socialism* (New York: B.W. Huebsch, 1913), 147-171.

10. Ibid., 157-158.

11. Mahatma Gandhi, "The Gospel of Swadeshi," accessed December 11, 2019, https://www.mk-gandhi.org/indiadreams/chap31.htm.

12. "Charkha," accessed November 6, 2019, https://mettacenter.org/definitions/charkha.

13. Wendell Berry, *The Long-Legged House* (Washington, D.C.: Shoemaker & Hoard, 2004), 87-88.

14. C.S. Lewis, *Surprised by Joy*, in *The Beloved Works of C.S. Lewis* (New York: Inspirational Press, 1998), 114. Lewis has defined chronological snobbery as "the uncritical acceptance of the intellectual climate common to our own age and the assumption that whatever has gone out of date is on that account discredited." In regard to this, he cautions that "our own age is also 'a period,' and certainly has, like all periods, its own characteristic illusions. They are likeliest to lurk in those widespread assumptions which are so ingrained in the age that no one dares to attack or feels it necessary to defend them."

15. Sōetsu Yanagi, *The Unknown Craftsman: A Japanese Insight into Beauty* (New York: Kodansha USA, 2013), 135.

16. Carlo Petrini, *Slow Food Nation* (New York: Rizzoli Ex Libris, 2007), 253.

17. All excerpts in this section from Borgmann, *Technology and the Character of Contemporary Life*, 200-205.

18. Wendell Berry, *Sex, Economy, Freedom & Community* (New York and San Francisco: Pantheon Books, 1993), 99-100.

APPENDIX A: TEAM PORTRAITS

APPENDIX B: THE RAFTER TAIL SYMBOLS

Kinga Kłusak

Eden Klein

Louis Jamin

Will Gusakov

Paul Cookson

Zakari LeBlanc

Asher Finch

Maxime Dumesnil &
Quentin Chevrier-Boré

Gustave Rémon

Loïc Desmonts

Michael Updegraff

Janne Aikonen

Andy Hyde

Sophie Wintzer

French Carpenter's Mark

Joshua A. Klein

Alicia Spence

Anonymous

Skip Dewhirst
& Eric Lion

Lizabeth Moniz
& Paul Cookson

Florian Carpentier

Miles Jenness

French Carpentry Numeral 9

Lizabeth Moniz

PHOTO CREDITS

All photographs by Joshua A. Klein except where noted.

FURTHER READING

Benson, Tedd. *Building the Timber Frame House: The Revival of a Forgotten Craft.* New York: Charles Scribner's Sons, 1980.

Berry, Wendell. *The Long-Legged House.* Washington, D.C.: Shoemaker & Hoard, 2004.

———. *Sex, Economy, Freedom & Community.* New York and San Francisco: Pantheon Books, 1993.

———. *What are People For?* New York: North Point Press, 1990.

Borgmann, Albert. *Technology and the Character of Contemporary Life.* Chicago: University of Chicago Press, 1984.

Calame, François. *Bouts de Bois - Bois de Bout L'atelier de Normandie/ European Carpenters Workshop in Normandie.* Die, France: éditions À Die, 2004.

———. *Charpentiers Sans Frontières: L'atelier de Normandie/ Carpenters Without Borders: Workshop in Normandy.* Caen, France: CRéCET, 2013.

Carr, Nicholas. *The Glass Cage: Automation and Us.* New York: W.W. Norton & Company, Inc., 2014.

Chesterton, G.K. *What's Wrong with the World.* 1910. Reprint, Mineola, NY: Dover Publications, Inc., 2007.

Coperthwaite, William. *A Handmade Life: In Search of Simplicity.* White River Junction, VT: Chelsea Green Publishing, 2007.

Crawford, Matthew B. *Shop Class as Soulcraft: An Inquiry Into the Value of Work.* New York: Penguin Books, 2009.

Csikszentmihalyi, Mihaly. *Flow: The Psychology of Optimal Experience.* New York: HarperCollins Publishers, 1990.

Forbes, Peter. *A Man Apart: Bill Coperthwaite's Radical Experiment in Living.* White River Junction, VT: Chelsea Green Publishing, 2015.

Gandhi, Mohandas. *Gandhi: 'Hind Swaraj' and Other Writings.* Cambridge: Cambridge University Press, 1997.

Garvin, James L. *A Building History of Northern New England.* Lebanon, NH: University Press of New England, 2001.

Gay, Craig M. *Modern Technology and the Human Future: A Christian Appraisal.* Downers Grove, IL: InterVarsity Press, 2018.

Gusakov, Will and Hank Silver. 2018. "Building Bridges with Charpentiers Sans Frontières." *Timber Framing*, December: 130.

Illich, Ivan. *Tools For Conviviality.* New York: Harper & Row, Publishers, 1973.

Lansky, Mitch, ed. *Low-impact Forestry: Forestry as if the Future Mattered.* Hallowell, ME: Maine Environmental Policy Institute, 2002.

Lisak, Will. 2018. "Carpentry Without Borders." *Mortise & Tenon Magazine*, Issue Four: 96.

Mumford, Lewis. *The Myth of the Machine: The Pentagon of Power.* New York: Harcourt, Brace & World, 1970.

Sale, Kirkpatrick. *Human Scale Revisited: A New Look at the Classic Case for a Decentralist Future.* White River Junction, VT: Chelsea Green Publishing, 2017.

———. *Rebels Against the Future: The Luddites and Their War on the Industrial Revolution.* New York: Addison-Wesley Publishing Company, 1995.

Schumacher, E.F. *Small is Beautiful: Economics as if People Mattered.* New York: Harper Perennial, 2014.

Sobon, Jack A. *Hand Hewn: The Traditions, Tools, and Enduring Beauty of Timber Framing.* North Adams, MA: Storey Publishing, 2019.

———. *Historic American Timber Joinery: A Graphic Guide.* Becket, MA: Timber Framers Guild, 2014.

Williams, Christopher. *Craftsmen of Necessity.* New York: Vintage Books, 1974.

Yanagi, Sōetsu. *The Unknown Craftsman: A Japanese Insight Into Beauty.* New York: Kodansha USA, 2013.

ACKNOWLEDGMENTS

I am immensely grateful to everyone who helped pull this project off: First and foremost, my indefatigable wife, Julia, for her support and enthusiasm in all our adventures together. There is no greater joy than to experience the grace of life with her. And I am constantly humbled by the adaptability and tenacity of my colleague, Michael Updegraff. His skills far outshine mine, yet he is always the first to volunteer for the trivial and weirdest of tasks we face at *M&T*: everything from thorny customer service inquiries to emptying the compost toilet buckets to burying rabid raccoons my neighbor shot.

The many contributing voices in this book fittingly reflect both the unity and diversity of *Charpentiers Sans Frontières*. Thank you to François Calame, Will Gusakov, Jason Breen, Andres Uus, Loïc Desmonts, Jordan Finch, Andy Hyde, Lizabeth Moniz, and Hank Silver for putting these thoughts to paper for us.

There were several people who worked with me behind the scenes to produce this book, all of whom I cannot thank enough. My editor, Michael Updegraff, slogged through the earliest drafts and gave me invaluable critique and direction. He also stuck it through to the end with me, ensuring no comma, conjunction, or italic was amiss. Jim McConnell, whose keen wordsmithing abilities enrich each issue of *Mortise & Tenon*, gave this manuscript the nip-and-tuck it needed at the final editing stages. My words always end up stronger once they've been nudged by Jim's red pen. Adam Spitalny and his designer's eye pushed me to greater intentionality as we weighed color, typeface, and layout selections. The beautiful presentation of this material is thanks to his astute sense of design. I am also thankful to my copy editor, Nancy Hiller, whose final review ensured that this presentation is as crisp and tidy as our readers deserve it to be.

And I am, of course, deeply indebted to all the carpenters who gave of their time and expertise to make this timber frame project happen. Working alongside them has been a tremendous gift to my family. Julia and I daily reminisce about our time together, and I am sure that my boys will never forget their kindness and warmth toward us. I would like to express particular thanks to François Calame, Will Gusakov, Hank Silver, and Will Lisak for organizing and planning such a complicated event in the midst of their professional and personal commitments. Not only were they the originators of this project, but they personally led it to fruition. I will never forget these 11 days we shared together.

The abundance of food we enjoyed came through the efforts of many hard-working and joy-filled souls:

The Kitchen Crew: Kinga Kłusak, Florence Calame-Levert, Lauren Cella, and Grace Cox.

The Farmers: Scott Pusey, Donna and Andy Birdsall, Jennifer Schroth and Jon Ellsworth, Amanda Provencher and Paul Schultz, Heather and Phil Retberg, and Peter Philbrook.

My deepest thanks are also due to many others who generously gave of their time, expertise, food, or other provisions:

Dennis Carter, Damian and Amy Bebell, Al and Mia Strong, David Dillon, Carrie Gray, Matthew Tunnessen, Tim Semler and Lydia Moffet, Carina Gressitt, Brittnay Reed, Hannah and Mike Nowell, Mike Cox, Cait and Dee Powell, Cindy Rankin, Matthew and Sherry Davis, Chara Grace Hamilton, Donna Tiemann, Paula Pusey, Deborah Hanson, Stephen Muscarella, Keyla Rodriguez, Angie Potter, Megan Updegraff, Sarah Pebworth, Julie Jo Fehrle, Wes Faulkenberry, George and Dawn Gans, Thomas Lie-Nielsen, Bill Schubeck, Heidi Daub, Fiona Schubeck, Ash Ngu, Tino Terrones, Cameron Turner, Hugo Baillargeon, Matija Hrkac, Mare Radic, Grigg Mullen Jr., David Quinby, Andy and Stephanie Klein, Troy and Allison Brown, Pilgrim OPC, Josh Wehrwein, and Kim Kopple and family.

ABOUT THE AUTHOR

Joshua A. Klein is editor-in-chief of *Mortise & Tenon Magazine*. He has been selected for the Early American Life Directory of Traditional American Crafts from 2015-2019 for his authentic approach to period furniture making, and has presented about historic craftsmanship at museums around the United States. He has written articles for *Popular Woodworking* and *American Period Furniture*, and his first book, *Hands Employed Aright: The Furniture Making of Jonathan Fisher (1768-1847),* was published by Lost Art Press in 2018. Joshua, his wife, and their three sons also maintain an active and growing homestead on the coast of Maine.

INDEX

Henrich groff moller

ICH